Roar: True Tales of Women Warriors

By 21 Women Writers

ISBN-13: 978-0692875766 (Better Said Than Done)

Preface

As a woman, I have heard many stories of womanhood. I will often be talking to another woman and she'll say, "And then he tried to kiss me. He's married!" And then we roll our eyes. Men. What can you do? Or she'll say, "Yeah, I didn't want to, but he didn't seem to want to take no for an answer," and then we roll our eyes, because, what can you do?

Workplace discrimination is common. I have heard stories from many women who've experienced it. Catcalling happens. Rape. Domestic violence. Sexual harassment. These things happen, all the time, to women.

What can you do? What we can do is speak up. I am not a man. I cannot speak for men. I can speak as a woman.

I developed the concept for this book late in 2016 when I felt an overwhelming sense of "What the heck?!" It seems like I have been having these conversations with women for forever. It seems like so many of us have experienced so much crap and that we all just roll our eyes and put up with it. And it seems like we are supposed to. That that is woman's work. Glossing over. Being okay with. Letting it slide. Playing nice. Mothering.

There are stories in this book to which many women will be able to relate. I have been there too. I'm with you, sister. There are stories in this book that are meant to inspire. Strong women, being powerful. There are stories in this book of heartbreak and regret that cry out for change. If only I hadn't. If only I could've. If only I did. Finally, there are stories in this book that are meant to illustrate – for any man or woman who hasn't been there. These women have. This happened to me. Let me show you what it was like, so you can understand.

Women have struggled for the equality we deserve, for equal rights, the same opportunities. Some would claim we've achieved that, that there is no reason for women to complain. Often, we don't.

Women are raised with a bias. Be nice. Play well with others. Don't upset anyone. Women are taught to be quiet. Be helpful. Be sympathetic. When that nice man at work, your boss, makes an inappropriate comment, just let it go. He didn't mean anything by it. When you have gone home with a guy you thought you liked, but feel uncomfortable now that you're alone in his apartment, don't upset him. He likes you. Just go ahead and smooth things over. If a guy you don't know tells you that you have a nice ass, say thank you. If a co-worker tells you that you look cute when you do math, just laugh. You know you're prettier when you smile. Be nice. Be quiet. Be a woman.

The 21 women in this book all have something to say about that. Whether their story is about taking care of a loved one, being a mother, or leaving an abusive relationship, they are not being quiet anymore. Neither should you. Keep talking to your friends when "he" does something. But talk to him, too. And them. And everyone. We shouldn't have to smile and smooth things over. We shouldn't be quiet. We are women. Let us roar.

Jessica Robinson
Better Said Than Done
April, 2017

All proceeds from book sales benefit The National Network to End Domestic Violence. The National Network to End Domestic Violence (NNEDV) is a nonprofit 501(c)(3) organization that serves as a leading national voice for domestic violence victims and their allies. NNEDV's membership includes all 56 state and territorial coalitions against domestic violence, including over 2,000 local programs. NNEDV has been advancing the movement against domestic violence over 25 years, having led efforts among domestic violence advocates and survivors in urging Congress to pass the landmark Violence Against Women Act of 1994. To learn more about NNEDV, please visit NNEDV.org.

This book was conceived, the stories were collected and the anthology was edited by Better Said Than Done. Better Said Than Done hosts monthly, themed storytelling shows in and around Fairfax County, Virginia. Our stories are true and personal. We also offer workshops for individuals and corporations as well as presentations on the art of storytelling.

Visit www.bettersaidthandone.com to learn more.

Table of Contents

Power Play

Anne B. Thomas

My boss, the President of the University, leans back in his chair, fiddles with his pen and says to me, "Bob tells me you are out to get Frank. Why would Bob say something like that?"

I stiffen at his question. Maybe because he's a sexist pig who is trying to protect a member of his good ole boy network? Forcing myself to relax, I look the President right in the eye and say, "I don't know why Bob would say that. You need to ask him. Did he share the results of my investigation into the complaints lodged against Frank?"

The President waves his hand in the air, dismissing my suggestion he actually look at the facts. "No. I don't have time for that." Of course not. That's how the good ole boy network thrives. We're important men who make important decisions. A confidential word of advice from one to the other is sufficient to cast aspersions. No need to examine the matter. We're men of integrity.

I'm the Civil Rights Officer for the University with 30,000 students, faculty and staff to protect – a contract position.

It's my job to respond to complaints of sexual harassment and other civil rights violations. I've just finished a doozy of an investigation into sexual harassment complaints against Frank, a branch campus director. The man should be fired, no question about it, and Bob, the Interim Provost, should be doing the firing. But he's raising questions about me instead.

As the number two executive at the University, Bob is much more powerful than me. Plus, he's a native of the state who has taught political science at the University for thirty years. He has many levers to push or pull to help or hinder the President's aspirations. The University is actively searching for a permanent provost. After today, that can't come soon enough.

On one level though, I think Bob's attempt to undermine me with the President is a good sign. He's feeling the heat and can't shut me down on his own, hence the interference from the President. But when I go home that night, I tell my husband about this new threat.

This is the mid-'90s and sexual harassment is still a relatively new anti-discrimination concept that is sending shock waves through certain men's sense of allowable workplace behavior. There is disbelief and resistance to the notion that it's wrong to compliment a woman on her good looks, crack a dirty joke or give an unasked-for shoulder massage.

The investigation into Frank all started when five staff from the branch campus came to my office to file a complaint about Frank's behavior. Ironically, it was Valentine's Day. Their leader, Jamie, a tall, bald man, shaped like a barrel, said, "We're all very nervous to be here. Can you promise us nothing bad will happen to us for talking to you?"

Sweeping my eyes around the room, I assure them, "Anything you say in here will be confidential. If you tell me about bad behavior, in violation of University policy, I have to act on it. But no one can punish you for coming to see me or filing a complaint."

Eyes flit back and forth among them, but Jamie nods his head at me and begins speaking again. "Our branch manager Frank is rude and crude. He insults the women on campus by leering at them. He pulls sexual pranks and thinks it's really funny, but it makes most of us sick. He has affairs on campus and asks us to cover it up so his wife won't find out. It's so bad we can't do our work. We all try and avoid him. We take circuitous routes at work to avoid having to run into him or take sick leave to avoid him altogether. These are good jobs in our small community. We don't want to risk losing them, but things are getting out of hand."

Five people coming at one time and corroborating each other in describing the director's behavior is significant.

These are big, serious allegations. I call my two investigators into the room and we all take notes as we ask follow up questions. Now our eyes flit back and forth at some of the salacious details they are sharing as we get a clear picture of the situation. After the meeting ends, we sit down and make arrangements to go to the branch campus to investigate their claims.

As we enter Frank's office to go over the complaints and begin the investigation, he gets up from behind his desk to greet us for the first time. His smile is a bit too wide and bright. A short man with slicked back blonde hair, he's wearing jeans, a light blue button down shirt and loose hanging tie.

He has a big office decorated with contemporary art, a messy desk and a ficus tree in the corner. I can't tell if it's silk or real. There are some award plaques on the wall and a glass spinning flame in recognition of igniting minds or something. Behind the desk is a large, picturesque window overlooking a bit of green with some bare willow trees.

He gestures to us to sit with him around the small round conference table in his office. I begin to tell him about the complaints, but he holds up a hand and says, "You're wasting your time. Everybody here is very happy. You can't let a couple of malcontents ruin things here."

In my most professional voice, I respond, "Of course. That's why we're here to determine if it is just the protestations of a few unhappy staff. So let's go through the allegations." I dive in. "The questions may sound harsh, but there's no way of sugar coating it either. Are you having an affair with your Director of Student Services?"

His face reddens, but he remains calm, "Of course not. That's a malicious lie."

I smile and continue. "Okay. Have you ever had any affairs with anyone who works at the branch campus for you?"

He leans back from the table, crosses his arms over his chest and says, "Why are you even asking me these questions? This is preposterous!"

He sounds a little too outraged to me and not the least bit surprised. "Part of the allegation against you is that you have affairs with your staff on campus. I'm just doing my job and giving you due process by informing you of the allegation and giving you a chance to respond to it."

He slowly drops his arms back to their sides. "I can't believe that I have to deal with this. You should know this is bullshit."

Ah yes, now he's attacking me, the questioner. I calmly reply, "The only way I can find out if it is untrue is by conducting an investigation. The University takes all complaints seriously. What is your response to that allegation? Have you had any affairs with any of your staff?"

He cocks his head to the side, brings his hand up so it blocks his mouth, and says, "No."

"Have you ever directed your secretary, or Assistant Branch Director, to lie to your wife about your whereabouts?"

Frank stares at me a good long minute. You don't intimidate me. I hold his gaze, keep my face neutral and wait him out. His eyes finally break away as he says, "No."

"Okay. Last Summer, did you acquire a very large bra, write 'Happy Birthday Grace' on the cups for one of your staff member's birthday and hang it, along with a large pair of women's panties, from the ceiling of the cafeteria?"

Frank pushes back in his chair, stands up, raises his arms wide to the side, and says, "Oh come on! That was a joke! Grace thought it was hilarious! She laughed loudest!"

"So you admit to doing that?"

Exasperated, he stuffs his hands in his pockets and says, "Yes. But this is so stupid. It was just a joke!"

"Grace is a large woman and she reports she was humiliated by that incident and begged you to take it down right away, but you refused."

Again the arms go out to the side, "Well that's what she said, but everybody thought it was hilarious, and then she laughed too. So really, she wasn't that upset."

"Moving on, in January, did you direct a security guard to purchase a box of condoms on University time?"

Frank stares at me again. But this time his eyes are wide, his face slack. I can practically hear him thinking, how the hell did she know about that? He sits back down. "He was making a bank deposit which is part of his job. The drug store was right next to the Bank."

"So you did ask him to buy the condoms for you?"

Leaning forward in his seat he says, "Why are you making a federal case out of everything? It's not a big deal. I paid for them. It took him maybe five minutes to run next store."

"After you received the condoms, did you then partially fill four or five of them with hand cream to make them appear used, and leave them on the hood of your 18-year-old work study student's car?"

Frank jumps up again, turns away from me, hands on hips, but I glimpse his red face and throbbing neck before his back is completely turned.

"What is this," he sputters, "the Spanish Inquisition?"

"No. This is the University doing its due diligence to a complaint of sexual harassment."

"Well I can see you're trying to twist having a little fun at work into something nasty. These little jokes build morale around here. I don't want a place that's all work and no play."

"Do you understand that this student was traumatized by your actions? She assumed the condoms had been used. She couldn't understand why her boss would do something like that and worried it was a sexual overture. Do you recognize that as the Director of this branch you hold a lot of authority and power over your staff?"

He turns back to face me. He softens his face and says, "We're a big, happy family down here."

I lay down my pen, take off my glasses and look directly at Frank, "I think the very fact I'm here is an indication that people are not happy here."

Jabbing a finger close to my face, Frank says, "You can't base your assessment of my branch on the complaints of a few troublemakers. Let me handle this."

This time I lean forward across the table, "Frank, you are beginning to sound dangerously like you would retaliate against the people who filed this complaint and that would be illegal. All staff are well within their rights to raise complaints about their managers and are protected against retaliation. Do not take any action against these people." Frank just stood there and fumed. He was not used to anyone interfering with his campus.

My staff and I then interviewed over thirty staff members and a few brave students. Frank's secretary admitted how awkward and uncomfortable it was to have to lie about Frank's whereabouts to his wife. Witnesses described how often he touched the women. We learned of three women he had affairs with; two were consensual, one was a single mother who did it to keep her job. There were filthy jokes and reports of eye sweeps up and down of women and students. Collectively, they painted a picture of a man drunk on power acting like a king who could do whatever he wanted. Away from the main campus without any direct oversight, there was very little to stop him.

I wrote up the report and made sure the depth and breadth of Frank's behavior was comprehensive and clear. I used direct quotes from witnesses, added up the number of staff that corroborated each allegation, provided an analysis of his behavior using the University's anti-sexual harassment policy language and gave the report to Frank's manager, Bob, for action. Clearly, he doesn't want to act. In part, he doesn't think these issues are that bad, but mostly he wants to take care of his friend. If he can't attack the contents of the report, he has to attack the author of it. Me.

Not only do we have disparate power levels, my work makes many people uncomfortable. They don't want to be investigated, they don't want me interfering in their hiring decisions to make sure we hire qualified minorities, they don't want to be scrutinized by statistics. I'm quite vulnerable to attack. It's the facts that always save me.

And now, the President is unwilling to read the report and learn the facts. I write a summary of our long report and give it to the President in hopes he can be enticed to read something shorter. I hear nothing. I write another report that lists every single University policy that Frank violated. No response. I tell him in a meeting that with the evidence we have uncovered, if we don't take appropriate action, we are vulnerable to a lawsuit. It doesn't matter. As Summer comes on, I can feel the heat of resentment from Bob and the President that I wasn't letting this matter drop and in fact was building a bigger record of the problem.

Professor friends tell me about off handed comments from Bob about my "over-zealousness" and "feminist" proclivities. When I raise the case with the President, he changes the topic. I know they're going to hire a new provost soon. I just hope I can keep my job until then – and I hope the new provost will be more reasonable than Bob.

I talk to my husband about what's happening at work. We look at our finances, figure out worse case scenarios, and cut back on expenses. I start looking for new employment opportunities in the state. Before my search, I knew this was a good job. After my search, I know it is the best job of its kind in the state. I don't want to lose this job. I shouldn't have to for doing what my job requires. In the three months since the meeting with the President when he asked me why Bob would say I was out to get Frank, I have developed insomnia. Sunday mornings I wake up with dread that I have a whole week of work ahead of me. I lose weight.

Finally, the President tells me, "I will not discuss this matter anymore. Drop it. I'm beginning to think Bob is right about you"

My contract says that the University has to give me three months' notice if they do not plan to renew my contract. As the date approaches, I worry that my persistence in this matter will actually cause me to lose my job, but I cannot stop pushing on it. These staff members trust me and risked everything to come forward and I'm sure Frank will find a way to make them pay for airing the branches dirty laundry if nothing happens to him.

And then the new Provost is announced; a woman. She's starting mid-August. Just two weeks before my contract renewal notice has to occur. I just have to hold on.

Per the President's direction, I don't raise the case about Frank, but the quality of our meetings are more tense, shorter, perfunctory. He rarely looks at me and stops asking for my advice. The number of meetings I'm included in diminish.

I practically hold my breath the last two weeks before the new Provost arrives, but I make it. Her second day on the job, I give her all three reports on Frank. The next morning, she calls me and says, "Is there any reason why we wouldn't fire this guy?" At last!

"Nope."

She must have told the President that I did good work because two weeks later, I sign my new one year contract. And a few months after that, Frank, having exhausted his internal appeal process, is packing up his office for a new branch director to take his place.

Love

Danielle Stonehirsch

It's 1998 and Amy and I sit on her parents' porch with two boys from the neighborhood on the swinging wooden benches back and forth up and down the four of us touching knees and pulling away back and forth up and down and I am almost happy because I love Amy and I love swinging but I do not love the boys who are tall with wide legs and long arms. I am 13 years old and my chest is heavy with air and my heart is fast but I know my chest is heavy and my heart is fast when there are people who are not Amy and I think this is okay, this is okay. A boy is sitting next to her and she is laughing and he is putting his face on her neck and she is putting her hand on his leg and a boy is sitting next to me and he is putting a hand on my leg and I am quiet because I am supposed to be making friends. My mother is worried I am not making friends and I am worried my mother is worried and I let the boy put his hand on my leg until he starts to move his hand and I say can you take your hand off my leg and he does not move his hand higher but he does not take it off and he says I thought you were from New Jersey. I am from New Jersey I tell him because I am and he says I thought girls from New Jersey like this and now I am not sure because maybe other girls from New Jersey like this and I am just not like other girls in New Jersey which I know because I have trouble making friends and that is why I am not in New Jersey anymore. I tell him I am sorry I am not like the other girls from New Jersey and he takes his hand away but I see he is angry and that he will not be my friend so I leave the swinging bench and walk through the house and into the backyard and I tell my mother we have to go and she tells me we can't go and I want to tell her about the boy and his hand but the boys' mother is there and my mother is happy so I walk through the house and into the front yard and sit on the swing and both boys sit next to Amy and move their hands on her legs.

It's 2002 and I can hear the rain on the windows and smell the bacon from the kitchen as the waiters rush back and forth, to and fro, in and out of the double silver doors. Amy sits across from me in the booth playing with the frosted smiley face cookies on the plate as the seconds roll by one after another after another. I twirl my fingers in my hair the way my mother tells me not to, you'll make yourself bald that way, she says, but I need it now like Amy needs her cigarettes, which she is always stepping outside for. I'm tugging on my hair and she's rolling the cookies across the table to the left to the right until one gets away from her and smashes on the floor. Now her palms are empty and she lays them on the table face up and I see on her forearms the marks up and down like polka dots like dimes like buttons on a doll dress. Whatever they are like, I know what they are and she knows that I know because I know everything. We know everything, and that's why when my eyes play connect the dots on her arms up to the stitches in her forehead I can't say what she wants me to say which is that it's okay, that it's all been okay, that it will be okay, and I am 17 years old and it's been a long time since I thought that everything might just might be okay. When she speaks she picks up another cookie to roll and she's not angry with me she's sad that I don't understand the complexities of love and I say love just sounds like a name you give to the reasons you let someone throw you at a radiator and she leaves with the cookie and for six months her parents can't find her, the police can't find her, I can't find her.

It's 2005 and he's gone he's been replaced and replaced again but nothing replaces the marks on her skin which simply multiply and when we sit across from each other in thc booth by the window near the double silver doors this time I don't know everything and she doesn't know everything and what we don't know presses against our chests as she plays with the cookies and I play with my hair and nothing and everything has changed. This is a rare moment this in person time this alone time and I want us to share all the things we can't share on the phone when he dials her calls when he answers her calls when he listens to her calls because he loves her, he loves her so much. I have formed my opinion on love from her and from those like her and I am 20 years old and I know that love is something women don't really need or want but I try to learn my lesson and smile because what I have learned is that when women are in love and they refuse to testify against the men who love them so much very little happens except that women who are not in love like me get cut off shut out thrown away and end up knowing nothing. Here I am in the booth and I ask her about New Orleans but she never went to New Orleans she went to Cleveland and she almost had a baby but then she didn't. I want to ask her about the baby but he's here now her ten minutes are over he's here and his eyes are blue and I know lots of eyes are blue but his eyes are the bluest eyes I have ever seen and I know I will never see blue eyes like his blue eyes and they make me feel as cold as the bluest thickest ice.

It's 2007 and I am in France I am making friends and my mother does not worry and my friends and I dance on Saturday nights in the city. On this Saturday night in the city I can see the speakers moving with the sound and feel my heart interrupted by the bass skipping over and over dancing with a boy who says you are beautiful you are sexy and I think this is good but when he puts his mouth on me and his hand on my leg I am not sure so I move back against the wall, there is always a wall, and he says I thought you are américaine and I say I am American and he says I thought girls from America like this. My heart is skipping and the speakers are moving and my friends are dancing with the boys and I let him move his hand because I am trying to make friends. He wants me to drink and when I do not drink he leaves, I leave, in the dark on the street in the summer the air is heavy on my chest and the bass still moves my heart skipping over and over until I do not hear them until they are around me until they say pretty girl pretty girl t'es si jolie and I don't look but to me their eyes are blue and I say please si vous plaît please don't touch me and they say how can we not touch such a pretty girl and my shame is always I do not fight I do not yell I shut my eyes against their blue eyes and say again please don't and say again please don't and say again please don't and my eyes are shut and my heart is skipping over and over and I am 22 years old and I know the marks they leave on my skin that only I can see look like polka dots like dimes like buttons on a doll dress.

It's 2010 and Amy is in Florida with a truck driver with a pilot with a policeman and she almost has a baby but then she doesn't. I am in St. Louis in Pittsburgh in Paris in Washington where I see so many women in love and I feel sick. I am drinking with boys and I am watching their movies and pretending to like their paintings and I am letting them put their hands in my hair. My hair is starting to fall out like my mother said but science points towards an underactive thyroid and it doesn't matter who is right because no matter what I lose, I am not in love and when they tell me they are in love I smile and tell them they are wrong, this is not love because we do not cry we do not fight we do not hurt each other I have no marks on my skin on my heart. Amy is engaged and then she is not and then she is engaged and then she is not and then she is engaged and then the truck driver the pilot the policeman are gone and when the fake diamonds fall out of the last ring Amy puts it aside and continues to look for love which she needs like cigarettes which she is always stepping outside for. Her hair is also falling out and I am 25 years old and all I really know is that thirty percent of women have under active thyroids and love is best avoided like cocaine in a bar toilet.

It's 2016 and Amy screens her phone calls and does not visit and all I see is Facebook Twitter Instagram pictures of sunsets pictures of beaches pictures of dogs and when she takes pictures of herself she holds the camera high above her head looks up smiling and the soft light hides the marks I know are there still on her skin and she is as she was the day on the swinging bench before she almost had a baby and then didn't. She is looking for love in the bars on the internet in the park she is looking, looking, looking, she cannot hear me anymore she has wandered so far. I have lunch with a man who tells me he is in love and I tell him you are not in love and he tells me I am wrong. He does not hit me he does not push me he does not press his lit cigarettes to my arm, he takes me to the circus he bakes me a cake he buys flowers for my grandmother and when I ask him to move his hand he does not tell me where he thinks I am from. I am in love but Amy is not there to see it and I cannot show her look do you see there are no marks on my skin and I answer my own phone but I am 30 years old and I know none of my words will ever fill the hole dug deep by cigarettes and the bluest eyes and I scroll through the pictures of the sunsets of the beaches of the dogs and I wish we knew everything and knew we knew everything.

Roar

A Psychic, An Alien, and A Secret

Erin Rodgers

I'm 18 years old and I'm at a Psychic Fair in Guelph Ontario. It's not something I'm particularly into, but the screamingly neon yellow flyer in the cafeteria made it seem like it could be fun. Also, I was trying to figure out an original birthday present for my dorm roommate. Anything to try to paper over the fact that she: an athletic, smart and popular cool girl is stuck for another four months sharing a tiny, cinderblock-walled room with me: an awkward suburban muppet of a girl with the street smarts of a container of Cool Whip.

The largest conference room at the Holiday Inn Guelph Hotel and Conference Centre is filled with a giant circle of folding tables draped in beach sarongs and speakers emitting slightly tinny, piped-in soundtrack of Enya. It does not seem like an ideal place for a metaphysical experience. But I'm already here, and I have an extra $50 from Christmas so I figure it's worth a shot.

My roommate peels off from me and confidently strides toward a table with a large crystal ball in the center. Even in picking psychics she is effortlessly self-assured. I, meanwhile, dither around until I find a table draped in the least beachy sarong, and, honestly, one that is $5 cheaper than all of the others. Because who says the spirits from beyond don't appreciate a thrifty choice?

I sit down in front of a no-nonsense woman wearing a bejeweled sweater. She smells of stale cigarette smoke and has a warm smile. Her hands, with their perfectly manicured French tip nails, slide my money towards herself and then to her husband who sits a foot away reading a well-worn paperback novel held together with packing tape. They spend five full minutes arguing like the old married couple they are about where he should put the money, in his wallet, or the cash box stowed under the table.

And I'll tell you, I don't know what I was expecting, but it's wasn't that.

When she finally begins, she presses play on a hissing cassette player to record my reading and begins to make a bunch of open ended statements about my future. "You will meet someone important soon. Great things are coming. It's important to believe in yourself." It's basically just a lot of kindly advice with the occasional dramatic hand gesture. Then, right before the reading is over she places one of her lightly callused hands over mine and looks me deep in the eyes. "There's something in you. It's not psychic abilities exactly, but it's something. It's some power inside you. Listen to it, it's very important."

My roommate and I leave the conference room, me uncomfortable and quiet, her chatting enthusiastically away about the twin daughters the psychic has predicted for her future. Maybe they will be with the guy that she is currently dating. He is a man who, due to his insistence on constantly flexing his arm muscles, enters through all doorways sideways. When I get home, I throw the cassette tape in the garbage.

I am twenty-two and sitting in the living room of my family's suburban home playing board games by candlelight. A blackout has shut off power to the Northeast and my Mom has insisted that I have to stay in "because who knows what is going to happen". She is convinced there will be a Mad Max Thunderdome level of possible anarchy involving lootings, violence and something she trails off before revealing. I look outside and see a white couple in matching polo shirts walking a golden retriever.

I spend a lot of time at home. For a month, every night after working at my job at a tiny and shiny jewelry kiosk at the mall I watch hours of television with my Mom. Most people I know go out and party, meeting new people, drinking and having the adventures that become the sex stories that they dazzle each other with at the food court the next day.

During these stories I mostly stay quiet, marveling at the ease at which they move through the world. I wonder how they do it as I watch them throw back their heads as they laugh. Their hair seems to glow, even in the dull florescent lighting.

The show my Mom and I watch is called "Roswell". It is about young people who are secretly aliens. I perhaps relate to it a little too much. I spend a lot of time thinking about Tess, the alien who has just arrived in Roswell who can't quite figure out how to talk to people.

Occasionally I go out, and my Mom recites all the possible dangers of the outside world before I leave the house. I understand, she's just worried about me. My younger brother Kevin died of Sudden Infant Death Syndrome when he was a baby. Her father died when she was a kid. There are no pictures of either of them, and they are almost never mentioned.

We don't talk about it but I know that these are things that have made her a worrier. They are secret hurts she doesn't talk about. They're there, they're just invisible, so I pretend not to notice them. I tell her about where I am going, I tell her what I am doing, I edit out the things she won't like.

I am two years old, my Mom has just lost my brother, Kevin, to a disorder that no one understands. She had a baby, and then, suddenly, she didn't. She is bathing me and I smile, "Don't be sad Mommy, I take care of you." This is the only story I know about this time. My Mom's stories go from when I am born to when I am about one and a half and then pick up again when I'm about four.

I am twenty-five and the children of my parents' friends all seem to be getting married. I am in a relationship that mostly consists of smoking pot, watching movies and not talking about emotions. It feels like PARADISE…mostly. Something inside feels wrong, but I ignore it and let everything continue on. My brain feels like it is stuffed with cotton balls. It's very soothing.

Well, until it is not and drags on for another year. In my weekly calls home, my Mom tells me about her friend's kids and their engagements and weddings and fancy jobs. I tell her about the improv shows I have done, editing out the hilarious and scene-organic boner joke that got a huge laugh. There is always a moment of silence on the line before she changes the subject. Every time I get off the phone my one-bedroom apartment feels a little bit smaller and I decide to keep my relationship going for a little while longer.

Eventually I attempt to trick my boyfriend into taking me to Ikea to let nature take its course. Instead, we break up three times in the course of a month.

After the third time, I know it's for sure done and I tell my Mom in our weekly call. She asks if he has found someone else and asks what I've done wrong.

In case you were wondering, your Mom asking if your ex has found someone hotter is one of those moments that really puts your life into perspective. That night I begin to refocus my efforts, start smoking less pot and writing more. I get a therapist. I even make a vision board on screaming neon yellow poster board. I throw it out in embarrassment a week later, but I do it.

I am thirty-three. I have a small business with my friend Nyree. My purse has business cards with my name on it. I no longer binge watch hours of reality shows through a cloud of bong smoke instead of doing work. Instead I binge watch hours of high quality reality TV like "Game of Arms" in between meetings. I am regularly surrounded by smart, kind, vivacious, funny people who probably all felt like aliens at one point. Friends and I spend hours talking about how to make the world better.

Nyree and I are excited to combine our events business with our political beliefs so we have created a panel event to get visionaries from across the city to share their ideas.

I sit behind a card table at a bar where I used to try to recapture the magic of that scene-organic boner joke I made that one time. I have a weird feeling in my stomach, but I pass it off as nerves.

My Mom arrives and I am excited for her to see the event that we've worked so hard on and distracted by all the day-of details. Before the event begins she storms silently past me. I know that I have done something to upset her but I'm not exactly sure what. I'm sure that as soon as the event starts and she hears the amazing speakers it'll all be forgotten.

The four speakers talk about their work and their life experiences. They talk about their shared struggles and how they affect their work. They talk about their peers and how regular people are changing our city for the better. They talk about how white privilege is something that Toronto feels uncomfortable with.

I hear my Mom whispering to the person beside her through most of the event. Suddenly my Mom strides over to me, snatches the piece of paper I am holding out of my hand and begins to write an angry screed. I know it's a screed because her always perfect handwriting is tilted slightly to the left. She wants me to make sure her questions are asked. I feel like a scolded child. The pile of business cards on the table looks pathetic now, as if I am a 4-year-old playing dress up. As she thrusts the paper into my hands, I rack my brain trying to figure out what has made her this furious. What did she hear that I hadn't?

The questions on the page include, "What about suburbs that don't have community centers?" and, "If I want to volunteer, I have to get a police check, who pays?"

By the way, my parents own a three-bedroom house in the suburbs. A police check costs $25. This is not a big financial concern. Also, who pays for the police check? The organization you are volunteering for. Done-zo.

After the event my Mom and I have the biggest fight we have ever had. An argument that seems to be about everything and nothing all at once. An argument that leaves my head swimming. Instead of her being proud of me and hugging me like in the movie I have created in my head, I chase after her down the street. She tells me we have nothing in common, that she doesn't understand me and that she can't do this anymore, turns on her heel and is gone.

I walk back into the event ugly crying like Leonardo DiCaprio in every movie he's ever been in (except for Wolf of Wall Street when only the audience was crying). I nearly slam straight into my friend Audra who has seen everything. She looks at me with kind eyes and asks me if I'm okay. My instinct is to say everything is fine, to make a joke, but before my brain can form anything my mouth says "My Mom might've just disowned me…um, and I think I'm kinda gay."

Audra smiles gently, puts a hand on my shoulder and says, "What if we put a pin in that second thing for now. One thing at a time, whattya say?" and hugs me.

I stand for a moment hugging one of my dearest friends, the sounds of conversation and "Rockin' Bar Tunes 8" or whatever it is that plays at bars fades into the background. I feel like I am 20 feet underwater.

What the hell did I just say? Where did that even come from? Oh my God, that was it. The "power" from all those years ago. I wasn't psychic, I was just GAY.

And I'll tell you, I don't know what I was expecting, but it wasn't that.

That night was the beginning of a lot of changes in my life. I actually talk about my feelings now and I spend a lot less time editing myself. I also haven't talked to my Mom in over a year.

Now don't get me wrong, I still love my Mom. She's my Mom. She's flawed and she can be hurtful but she'll always be my Mom and in her own way she loves me. She's a person who has dealt with loss that I can't even imagine, partly because we've never talked about it. She's not evil. I mean, when she came to my panel she was wearing a jacket made of Dalmation puppies, but that's just a style thing.

But I've realized something – you can love someone and they may not be able to love you back in the way you need. Even if they're family. And maybe even though you're not the person they envisioned, they can love the person you are. And that editing and recreating parts of yourself to what you think someone else wants means that you'll never know if they can.

Just in case I understood that psychic wrong all those years ago and I do have a touch of clairvoyant power, I'd like to leave you with a vision. It's the summer of 2020 and I'm walking hand in hand with my partner in a beautiful tree-lined park. She's a social worker with a kind smile, a great sense of humor and a strong working knowledge of "Golden Girls" episodes. We have a small dog named Cheeseburger who is sweet, and small and emphatically not a pug because they are a ridiculous breed that does not actually function as dog.

We pull out a picnic blanket and start putting out food for everyone. And maybe my Mom is there. And maybe she isn't. But I do know that we'll be surrounded by family. Because me, the real me, the me that I am now, is always surrounded by incredible chosen family. Family that love me just how I am.

Trail Markers in the Wilderness

Elizabeth Futrell

Middle school is full of mortifying moments. At least one of mine, though, was prophetic. We were boarding the school bus home from a field trip to the Robert Crown Center for Health Education, rowdy after spending the better part of the day immersed in serious lectures and cringe-worthy videos about reproductive health and the dangers of drugs and alcohol. Each year's class visit to Robert Crown prompted a hormone-driven blend of dread, eye rolls, dramatic sighs, and incessant giggles.

I sat down on the bus with my three best friends, and we started a game of "Most likely to…" After going several rounds, we landed on the killer question: "Who's most likely to work at the Robert Crown Center when they grow up?"

The mere thought that any of us could work at a place like that – the source of so much embarrassment among Chicagoland tweens– was horrifying.

"Liz!" "Liz!" "Oh yeah. Definitely Liz!"

My face burned. Everyone around us was laughing, nodding in agreement. At least half the bus had overheard this mortifying prediction of my future, and I squirmed under the crushing weight of their easy and unanimous decision. What was it about me that made them think I'd end up talking about sex for a living?

***

A young Catholic married couple led the youth group my parents forced me to attend throughout high school. The name of the program was Godparents, and the idea was that George and Kelly played the role of Godparents, or trusted adult confidantes, to us. At 27, they had two young children and a third on the way.

Every Sunday night, we would gather at their modest suburban home to discuss issues of faith, religion, and teen life in general. Sex would occasionally come up in conversation. Each time it did, George and Kelly would gravely caution us that anyone who had premarital sex would go to hell (unless, of course, we confessed our sin and asked for forgiveness, which seemed easy enough). That was the extent of our conversations on the matter. And that was more than most of us had heard about sex in our Catholic homes from our parents.

Junior year, one of the girls in our group gave birth to a baby girl.

Senior year, a second group member got pregnant.

By the time I graduated, quite a few of my classmates had gotten pregnant, and I had seen friends through pregnancy tests, abortions, miscarriages, adoptions, baby showers, and births.

For some of us (my high school boyfriend and I included), watching our peers try to navigate these grown-up situations at 15 or 16 years old was very effective birth control. But for others, the feeling that everyone else was having sex magnified the pressure to follow suit.

I remember attending a birthday party my sophomore year for two seniors who were dating. As a gift, their friends were sending them to Sybaris, a suburban "couple's retreat" that boasted pool suites and rooms for rent by the hour. My boyfriend and I gave our friends a big box of condoms with a bow on top. It was the first time we had ever bought condoms, and I still remember the terror I felt as the pharmacist asked how he could assist us. At the party, though, we were cool and nonchalant, as if we were simply sharing our stash with them. I'd be tempted to believe that many of us had been less sexually active than we let on, except for the memory of watching nine of my friends' bellies grow and grow that year until they left school to have their babies.

What I didn't see was the actual parenthood that followed. I went away to college and then further away to the Peace Corps and so on. Now, while I'm chasing around my preschool-age daughters, a fair number of my high school classmates have adult children. I'm willing to bet that at least one or two people from my graduating class are 38-year-old grandparents.

The final youth group meeting before graduation is stuck firmly in my memory. We sat in a circle in the living room as George and Kelly shared their impressions of us, and their hopes for our future.

When it was my turn, George said, "Liz, you're the intellectual of the bunch. We love that you ask questions and seek deep answers. But we worry that your intellect puts you at risk because it might allow you to choose reason over faith and rationalize things like contraception."

I thought it was such a strange choice to use contraception as an example of the "danger" of my intellect when we had two teen mothers in our midst.

Two teen mothers who, however hard they worked and however smart and strong they were– and they were – would likely never have the same educational and economic opportunities in their young lives that I would have.

It turns out my Godparents' cautionary advice was prophetic, too. Sometimes I smile and think, "If they could see me now…"

***

On September 11, 2001, I was just two weeks into my teaching career in suburban Chicago. I spent the morning planning period in the school's audio-visual room, watching in horror as the Twin Towers fell and the Pentagon smoldered.

At the end of the last period of the day, one of my quieter ninth grade students, Mae, gave me a handwritten note on a folded piece of notebook paper. "Don't read it until after I leave, okay, Miss Ward?" And she darted out of the classroom.

The long note described, in bubbly 14-year-old-girl handwriting, how Mae's stepfather's 37-year-old friend had been having sex with her. It was clear in her note that she had felt during the relationship that it was consensual and romantic. But someone had found out and told her parents, and the gravity of the situation was dawning on her. Now Mae would have to face her predator in court and testify against him, and she was terrified. She didn't trust any of the adults in her life to keep her safe. And so, on a torn piece of notebook paper, she begged me to help her. The contents of this note, against the surreal and horrific backdrop of 9/11, were almost too much to bear. But while the events unfolding on the national and global stage that day left me feeling paralyzed with grief and fear for our country, Mae's note propelled me to act immediately on her behalf. In a time marked by such strong feelings of helplessness, it felt good to actually be able to help someone.

When I took the note to the school's administration, I was grateful for their compassionate and proactive response. They set Mae and me up in an official mentoring program for students dealing with trauma and abuse. We were able to spend time alone together and talk. She needed a grownup to listen to her. To help her define her limits, her expectations, and herself.

Several years later, I began teaching at a new high school in North Carolina. The scant teacher orientation included the strict directive that we were not, under any circumstances, to discuss sex or other sensitive subjects with our students. I was new to the South and didn't know if the policy of sweeping sensitive matters under the rug was unique to this particular school or whether it was typical. But it was one of my first glimpses, through adult eyes, of what happens when the institutions that are supposed to equip youth to thrive in this world willfully ignore their needs.

My fourth period class of ninth graders that year was troubled and challenging. Once I assigned them narrative essays about an experience that had shaped their perspective on life. They wrote about things like seeing a friend gunned down in a drive-by shooting, attempting suicide, experimenting with sex, and taking pregnancy tests. And I wasn't supposed to discuss any of it with them. When I was a student, I never would have dreamed of telling my teachers this stuff. But many of these kids had little support or structure at home, and they were desperate for someone – whether a person or an institution – to care about their reality, to expect something of them, and to establish boundaries for them.

***

By the end of that school year, I was ready to change careers. After spending a couple of years teaching overseas, I found it hard to readjust to the American educational system. I wanted to do more international work and maybe focus on social work or public health, interests that had been sparked in college by volunteer work I did with people living with HIV and AIDS. While I tried to determine my next career move, I took a corporate administrative job. Thinking it would be a good way to see if I was cut out to be a social worker, I signed up to volunteer as a financial literacy mentor for a local program that aimed to help low-income women gain financial independence.

I was paired with a woman named Shania who was recovering from addiction. At age 34, she had six children and one grandchild. She'd had her first child at age 12. He was in prison. She had her second child at 16. She didn't know where he was. Her four youngest children lived with her, having survived sexual abuse by her ex-husband, who was now in prison. Shania's daughter DeeDee, now 14, had given birth to a daughter at age 12.

Every three months, Shania would take DeeDee on the long bus ride to the clinic to get a Depo Provera shot, a contraceptive regimen she started just after giving birth. I asked Shania if she also got a Depo shot. (One condition of participation in our program was that the women could not be pregnant.) "Nah," she said. "It's not for me."

I began spending more time at Shania's apartment, which was provided by the mentoring program. I helped her create a budget and prepare to take her driver's test. Her kids sat around us, jumping in with answers, excited that their mother might be able to procure a license and a car with the money she was saving from her new job at a dry cleaner. As I watched Shania interact with her kids, I saw that they watched and worried over her, and not the other way around.

Before long, things started to go downhill. I took an afternoon off of work to take Shania for her driver's test. She failed. We practiced more and returned to the DMV.

She failed again. Her kids had learned the material inside and out, but she struggled. She never got her license, but she had nevertheless taken the small amount of money she had saved up from her job and used it to buy a barely-functional minivan. Then she lost her job at the dry cleaners. The program helped her get another job at a thrift store, but to get there, she had to take several buses, making for a two-hour commute each way. Another woman in the program who worked at the thrift store told me that things weren't good there. She thought the store manager was dealing crack.

Shania's belly began to grow. The program supervisors grilled her about whether she was pregnant and made me do the same. "Hell no," she said, "And thanks for making me feel fat!"

Shania lost her job at the thrift store. Though she adamantly denied it, she was struggling again with her crack addiction. And she was, in fact, pregnant – with twins. Because pregnancy was a program violation, she was expelled. This meant she lost her transitional housing.

She and her four children and her one grandchild and her two unborn children were going to be homeless.

After that, I decided not to mentor anyone else. I felt guilty for having been blind to what was really going on with Shania – for helplessly saying goodbye to her kids as they separated and scattered to unstable living situations and uncertain futures. I knew then that I was not cut out for social work. Someone from the program called me a few months later to let me know that Shania's babies had been born. They were one pound each.

***

If I hadn't been able to obtain a prescription for birth control pills at my university's campus health center as a college student; if I hadn't been able to access the morning after pill just out of college after a bad night; if I hadn't been able to rely on Planned Parenthood for routine exams and contraception in my low-income days as a newly returned Peace Corps Volunteer and an underpaid North Carolina teacher– I, too, might have been a young mom. And if I had, I probably wouldn't have gotten to spend my twenties teaching in North Africa and Asia, attending graduate school, and pursuing creative endeavors. I may not have had the chance to find and marry my true partner, and I certainly wouldn't have the professional or economic opportunities I have now. Those limits would have altered not just my own experiences and opportunities, but those of my children.

When kids think about what they want to be when they grow up, they're only aware of a small fraction of the careers that exist. Teacher. Nurse. Firefighter. Baker. Since I knew I didn't have the stomach to be a doctor or a nurse, it never occurred to me that I could work in family planning and reproductive health—that I could take the ability to empower people with knowledge, which I had honed as a teacher, and apply it to public health.

I lucked into the field through an internship during graduate school and eventually landed at the Johns Hopkins Center for Communication Programs working on the Knowledge for Health (K4Health) Project, which aims to ensure that family planning program managers and health service providers in low- and middle-income countries have access to the most up-to-date guidance and tools to help them serve their clients effectively.

I'm one of the lucky few who actually loves my job. A couple of years ago, my colleagues and I launched Family Planning Voices, a global storytelling initiative in support of contraceptive access. My work on the initiative includes interviewing fascinating people all over the world about the work they do and why they do it.

Many of the people I've interviewed tell harrowing stories of the difference between life and death that access to reproductive health services like contraception can make, especially in low-resource settings. Though I've lived and worked in several countries, I haven't seen firsthand the dire circumstances many of my colleagues have faced regularly: women dying in childbirth under the strain of being too young to give birth or having given birth too many times; frightened girls bleeding to death after unsafe abortions; undernourished babies and children. But sitting down with diverse people from around the world, from midwives to high-level donors to young advocates, makes me realize that each of us has a compelling story, a path that led us to this work.

For some of us, it is only in hindsight that we're able to see we were on a path at all.

Five Ounces of Milk

Sandra Hull

I used to wish my parents had hit me.

If they had, there'd be visible scars or maybe a permanent injury that would give insight into my introverted, self-effacing personality masking an ever-simmering anger that flared up without warning. It would explain the emotional repression and social anxiety that long kept me closed tight in a cocoon of shame, believing I wasn't worthy to try the wings that were my birthright.

I *had* managed a fledgling flight in my late 20s, landing 400 miles away in Washington DC. Everything seemed to be working out for me at first – a new life in a new and exciting city and a dream job in Georgetown, using my graduate studies in French to help launch the US office of a Bordeaux-based engineering services firm. There were just two of us, me and my French-born boss. We clicked immediately and functioned amazingly well as a team – until our home office suddenly cut our original 3-year startup timeframe down to 1 year without allotting us any additional cash or other resources. My boss began to blame me for every setback as we struggled to meet the impossible new deadline, yelling at me in French with the occasional English "goddammit" thrown in. Intellectually, I knew that he was projecting his own anxiety and failures onto me but, emotionally, I accepted that it was indeed all my fault, silently enduring my boss' tantrums with an apologetically bowed head.

When this began to affect my personal life in the form of debilitating insomnia, I went to a therapist who specialized in stress management. I didn't want my lack of sleep to hamper my work performance and further fuel my boss' wrath. The therapist spent our entire first session quizzing me about my childhood, overriding my objections that my problem was with my boss, not my family. At the beginning of the second session he told me that my parents were emotional bullies who had effectively groomed me to be victimized by my boss.

I shook my head. "That's impossible. My parents weren't abusive. They always told me they loved me!"

He remained silent, watching me with kind eyes while I reviewed my answers from the previous session and did the math. The resulting truth landed on me like a punch in the gut.

Anyone who met my parents socially would likely never guess how this witty, intelligent, charismatic couple with "caring" professions – Dad was a minister and Mom was a pediatric nurse – treated their children and each other when no one other than the immediate family was around. Belittling insults, mean-spirited teasing, and name calling disguised as humor. Psychological sleight-of-hand and gaslighting galore: what we heard them say wasn't what they'd said; what we saw them do never really happened; what vivid imaginations we had! The internet was still a few decades away yet it was the equivalent of growing up trapped in a comment thread populated by toxic trolls.

It was death by a thousand cuts – random incidents that, taken individually, didn't appear to be deliberately hurtful. Mom and Dad managed to dole out just enough praise and affection to maintain an illusion of normalcy. Any semblance of dysfunction was just our imagination.

Everyone in our household was fair game for abuse but each parent was slightly less hard on their own personal favorite, their own golden child. My mother doted on Younger Brother, who closely resembled her side of the family. My father favored Older Brother, who was pretty much his Mini-Me. The favoritism was even hard-wired into my brothers' names. Older Brother's middle name is Dad's first name. Younger Brother's middle name is the masculine form of Mom's first name. As the middle child, and only girl, I wasn't named after anyone. I was no one's favorite and everyone's scapegoat. In the family's ongoing game of emotional Russian roulette, I nearly always drew the loaded chamber.

It was drilled into me early on that if I was upset by being treated badly I was either overreacting, had misinterpreted the situation, provoked it, or otherwise had it coming. On the other hand, if I treated someone else badly it was because I was selfish and cruel. Intellectually, I knew this was unfair but my spirited protests were peremptorily shot down so often that I eventually internalized the anger, stopped protesting and simply accepted the blame. Resistance was futile so why bother?

My doormat days had begun.

The worst moments came during dinner. It was pretty much the only time we were ever all together as a family unit. The dining room table served as a circular stage for nightly theater of cruelty starring me as the featured victim. A particularly memorable performance was triggered by something ordinary: milk.

My mother strictly rationed milk in our household. Her inviolate rule was one glass of milk per person per meal. Period. I no longer remember the reason why. In retrospect, weighted with the wisdom of middle age, it occurs to me that Mom rationed milk as a means of control. It's common for abuse victims to find someone weaker than themselves to dominate. Dad abused her the same way he did us kids. He'd belittle her in front of us, telling us we didn't have to listen to her. She suffered a broken rib once when he "hugged her too hard."

By the same token, Older Brother picked on me using the tactics our parents modeled and when my simmering internalized anger would occasionally reach a boiling point, I likewise lost control and broke out of doormat mode to pick on Younger Brother. Any temporary psychological reward was always outweighed by guilt because I could see I hurt Younger Brother as much Older Brother hurt me. Additionally, I almost always got punished for it, whereas Older Brother never did.

One evening when it was Younger Brother's turn to set the table and pour the milk, he put the smallest glass in the house – a 3-ounce double shot glass – at my place, thereby giving me the drinkware equivalent of the middle finger. Everyone else had their usual 8-ounce glass. The defiant payback gesture wasn't lost on me, but I was confident it would backfire. No way could this glass that was no bigger than a sample-size bottle of shampoo be seen to count as my allotted milk ration. I felt certain that logic and fairness were on my side; I had at least one refill coming. Nice try, little bro, but you're gonna lose this round.

Of course, my glass was emptied early in the meal. With a sneer in Younger Brother's direction, I asked Mom for more milk. She laughed – at me, not with me – and shook her head. "Absolutely not. You know the rule: one glass of milk per meal." I held up the tiny glass and pointed out that it held less than half of what everyone else's did.

Again, she laughed and again she said no. Her eyes twinkled with delight and her mocking expression conveyed that she knew how silly it was to deny my request but at the same time she wasn't about to grant it either. Logic and fairness had abandoned me on the battlefield.

The word "schadenfreude" most certainly wasn't in Younger Brother's second-grade vocabulary but his gleeful laugh signaled it was clearly in his heart. Older Brother smirked at me. I turned to my father, the minister whose favorite Bible quote was the one about clothing the naked and feeding the hungry, hoping he'd intervene on my behalf if for no other reason than to undermine my mother.

Nope. He laughed in my face. "Ha, ha, you blew it!"

A frisson of despair flashed across my gut. There was no one left to turn to. I was surrounded by my family yet I was completely alone, humiliated. My family was mocking me for both asking for and having been denied five ounces of milk. To compound my sense of utter defeat, I realized that had I been the one to give Younger Brother the tiny glass he would've received an immediate refill with no questions asked and certainly with no mocking, while I would've been punished for slighting him. My inner rebel wanted to grab the carton of milk and refill my glass but my inner doormat knew the gesture would only beget more mocking and certain punishment. I bowed my head in shame and forced the rest of the meal down my dry throat.

Armed with this memory and countless others like it, it only took a handful of sessions for my therapist and I to deconstruct the systematic emotional abuse that started in my childhood and continued long after I'd reached adulthood. Knowing that I finally had an ally, I began to replace self-doubt and shame with self-love and assertiveness. My cocoon of shame finally began to crack open. I was freed – to unfold my wings and let them take me wherever I felt like going, not where anyone else told me to.

One of the first places I went was to a new job, away from my foul-mouthed francophone boss.

It was the beginning of the end of my doormat days.

Roar

Perseverance

Urmilla Khanna

Growing up in India at a time when very few girls went to college my father was determined to educate me. He encouraged me to set my goals high. I chose the medical profession. Most women who entered healthcare in those days became aides or nurses. They touched men and cleaned up after them, a taboo for a Hindu girl, the daughter of a well-respected engineer in the Indian Civil Service. On the other hand, a doctor was considered dignified, and I received all the support I needed. However, what would happen once I completed my education was in limbo. Girls from privileged families rarely worked outside their homes. As soon as they finished their education, they were married off to a man of equal or better status. They were surrounded by servants and lived comfortable lives. Whether I would be able to work after I graduated, I was told by my parents, depended on the views of the family that I married into.

My own formative years were greatly influenced by the British Raj. Studying in a convent school surrounded by European nuns and later training in an American mission hospital, I developed a mind of my own. I wanted to graduate and serve the sick and needy. Unlike most professional women who spent their lives in spinsterhood, I desired to marry. My dreams grew along with me and I began to yearn for a home, a family and a career in medicine. I became obsessed with going to America – the land of scientific discoveries and job opportunities. If only I could get there, I thought. It will free me from the choking atmosphere of customs, castes and hierarchy.

When I finished my medical degree and returned home to talk about my future, I discovered a deep chasm between my parent's views and my own. Whereas they had been liberal regarding my education, their plans for my future were indisputable – I must accept an arranged marriage. After innumerable battles with them and struggles with my own youthful desire to marry someone of my own choosing, I succumbed to their wishes. Confused, embarrassed and at times fearful, I finally went along with the age-old custom of bride showing. My name appeared in the matrimonial column of Times of India and other newspapers. And when the responses came in, I played my role of serving tea to each prospective groom in a formal setting. After several such encounters, and almost two years of a futile hunt, I was introduced to Kris, a Punjabi youth finishing his doctorate in the United States. He was in India for a three-month holiday, determined to find himself a bride. Whether it was love at first sight or karma, he expressed his desire to marry me. His credentials were impressive and my parents assured me that he came from a loving family. Still ambivalent about how arranged marriages work, I agreed to marry him. Ten days after a big Punjabi wedding, I was in America living with a stranger who was also my husband and guessing what his views might be towards a professional wife.

The year was 1963. Adjusting to my new life was challenging and exciting. Our love and respect for each other grew and so did my confidence in arranged marriages. To make my marriage work, however, I offered to follow my husband wherever his job took him. After a year in Connecticut, we returned to India. I spent my time running a home, raising our two boys – born fifteen months apart – and taking part-time jobs in basic sciences when possible. My disappointment in not being able to pursue my profession in America stayed locked up inside me.

Dissatisfied with Kris's job prospects in India, we were back in America in 1968, this time for good. My yearning to return to clinical medicine resurfaced. My husband had joined the faculty in the school of public health at the University of Michigan in Ann Arbor, Michigan. He was training to become an environmental toxicologist. Although I had a degree in pediatrics from India and two years of clinical experience, I had to start from the bottom up. I needed two years of pediatric residency from an accredited hospital to take the pediatric boards and get a license to practice medicine. And to enter a residency program, I needed to clear the Educational Commission for Foreign Medical Graduates (ECFMG) – a tough exam.

The first thing to do therefore, was to find my way into the working world. After several discouraging enquiries, I received a call from Dr. Carr, director of the department of clinical pharmacology at the university. "The opening is for a lab technician's position. You will be over qualified and underpaid," he said. I needed to get into an atmosphere of learning. Then I could study for the ECFMG exam. I decided to go for an interview.

I was dressed in a sari when I appeared for my interview. Dr. Carr seemed surprised as he looked at me and he fumbled for words. My sari could be a public hazard due to the radioactive materials I may be working with and my long hair, a hazard to myself in the laboratory. If I wanted the job, he said, I would need to conform to their dress code. Of course, I wanted the job. However, I was quite surprised at his perspective about the dress code. No one had given a second thought to my attire when I had worked in India. Now, I was in America and I needed to follow their customs. Leaving my heritage behind, I entered a boutique dress shop in my sari and emerged Mary Tyler Moore style wearing a pleated skirt and a turtleneck blouse. My long braids of silky black hair sat on my dresser in a Ziploc, a memento of my success story.

Dr. Carr soon promoted me to the position of a fellow and offered me a two-year scholarship for a master's degree in clinical pharmacology. I could not believe how well my life was shaping. I was being paid to study. It was all in my karma, I told myself. I worked in the laboratory until noon, took classes in the afternoon, and studied in the library after dinner. In fifteen months, I completed the requirements for my master's and had also passed the ECFMG. I quit my pursuit of basic sciences and began to look for a residency in pediatrics. My children were older and I was ready to take that plunge. I knew exactly what it would entail. I had done it once in India.

With multiple letters of recommendation, both from the professors I had worked for in Ann Arbor, and from the faculty with whom I had trained in India, I sent my resume to the Ann Arbor Medical Center in Ann Arbor. I was called for an interview by the chief of pediatrics, Dr. Oliver. I walked into his office with hope. I was qualified and was prepared to work hard. I saw no roadblocks.

My interview with Dr. Oliver stays in my memory as if it was yesterday. I was sitting across from him in a brightly lit room.

"I see that you come with strong recommendations. You appear intelligent and you interview well," he said as he made small talk and turned the pages in my file. He commented on my command of the English language.

I smiled. My thoughts jumped forward. I saw myself as a board-certified pediatrician in a matter of two years. Then, Dr. Oliver's tone changed and I felt a stab in my stomach. He enumerated the reasons that would disqualify me from his program. Starting by ejecting his thumb from a tightly closed fist, he counted the strikes against me. "You are a woman," he said. "And a happily married woman at that; a divorcee with children to support may merit a consideration." My jaw fell. I pursed my lips and swallowed. I thought of my loving family at home. My success in marriage was working against me.

Then he presented his index finger, "You are from India." I imagined him viewing me as a peasant girl living in a thatched hut with cows roaming in the streets around me. His objections continued. "You are brown. What young mother would allow you touch the belly of her precious newborn?" He did not expect an answer. He was on his fourth objection. "You have been away from clinical medicine for seven years?" My eyes met his and I nodded ever so slightly. "There have been so many new developments and a lot has changed. You can never catch up and compete with my young graduates." I wanted to point out to him that I had worked in related sciences all those years and was keeping up with the latest literature. I had also passed the comprehensive ECFMG exam. Instead, I recoiled into my cocoon. His words became a resonating noise and my vision blurred. I saw him put his little finger forward and heard his fifth and final blow. "You want to train in Ann Arbor not because it is a great university but because it is convenient for you. I see that your husband is a post-doctoral fellow at the university." He looked at my resume and then at me. His defiant stare and a long pause made me believe that he was waiting for me to say something.

"Yes, sir," I uttered in a choking voice.

I was thankful that he had just five fingers. Our meeting ended and with it, my hopes. I suppressed my tears and walked out of his office. With my head spinning, I recounted my encounter with Dr. Oliver. I touched the skin on the back of my hand. Maybe he has a point. When I was a child I used to read stories in British magazines where we the locals were depicted as subhuman savages lacking in intelligence. White supremacy entrenched into my core surfaced in my mind. I am not prone to anger but that day I felt intimidated. I wanted to give up and go back to India. But then again, that was not an option. I was an American citizen.

Time was a healer, and encouragement from my husband, a blessing. In a few weeks, I secured a residency at the

University of Toledo, in Toledo, Ohio. This, however, came at a price. I had to give the hospital one extra year of service by joining as an intern. This extended my training to three years rather than the required two. "Beggars cannot be choosers," my father used to say.

It was gratifying to work with patients again and life fell into a pleasant routine. Rain, snow or shine, I drove the sixty miles each way and signed in at seven-thirty each morning. I took night calls every third night, and when short on help, every other night. My exhilarated spirits compensated for the physical exhaustion. "I have never seen you so happy," Kris said to me one Monday morning when I came home after a long three-day weekend at the hospital. During my absence, he pitched in every way possible. He had the children, then five and six, fed, bathed and ready for school on time. On weekends, he took them on long hikes, collecting rocks and wild flowers. I missed these family times, but it was a tradeoff that I had chosen.

I had been working in Toledo for about fifteen months when I decided to take a short vacation. Our parents were aging and Kris and I had an urge to see them. We went to India for three weeks and had a joyous holiday. Our families were delighted to see us and hear about our success stories. "You are moving up the ladder. May god bless you, always." my father-in-law said. With these words ringing in my ears, I felt rejuvenated and energized to complete my residency.

When I returned to America, a new setback awaited me. Among the mail that had accumulated while we were away, there was a letter from Dr. Rejent, acting chief of pediatrics in Toledo. It stated that my position as a resident had been terminated. Reason: I had left without my leave being sanctioned. I felt as if I was drowning in a bottomless sea. I had spoken to Dr. Rejent about my desire to take a break and visit my family. "Let me know when you firm up your plans," she said. However, by the time my travel papers came through, she had left on a month's vacation. In her absence, my leave was approved by Dr. Brookfield, chief of the residency program.

I approached Dr. Rejent to explain the situation but I was not given a chance to speak. She was the only one who sanctioned leave for residents, she said. And her word was final. I had been taught by my parents to look up at the angrezi-log – the white race of British India. Honest, hardworking and fair, they were my role model. My childhood image was shattered. Dr. Rejent's authority was unreal and yet, I had to accept this paradox and move on. I walked out of the hospital feeling small and insignificant. I was being tried for a crime I had not committed. With tears rolling down my cheeks, I questioned my karma.

I had become accustomed to working eighty or more hours a week. Now, I woke up each morning and saw a bleak future and the stigma on my resume. A few months earlier I had paid the fee for taking my pediatric boards. Instead of letting gloom take over my life, I returned to the library.

When I learned that I had passed my boards, I had a longing to share the good news with Dr. Rejent. In the six months that had passed she could have had a change of heart. I remembered the times when she used to refer to me as one of her favorite residents. With that optimism, and all the courage I could muster, I called her office. I learned that the temporary position held by Dr. Rejent had been filled by Dr. Torres and that she had left the department. I took a deep breath. I would now be dealing with a new chief who knew nothing about me except what he saw in my resume. With trepidation, I made my appointment.

When I walked into Dr. Torres's office and saw the familiar manila folder on his desk, I cringed. I was searching for words to tell him my side of the story, when he interrupted me. "I know, I know," he said. "I am an immigrant too, and I understand. From what I see, it was all internal – nothing to do with you." His placid countenance and soft-spoken demeanor made my eyes well with emotions. Once again, I regained my faith in humanity.

It was June, the month when residents are interviewed and vacancies filled. I joined the new residents and completed the remaining months of my training. In 1974 I was certified to practice medicine in America. It can all be done with patience, perseverance and determination, although karma could play an important role.

Roar

Mother and Daughter: Decisions Made in Grief

Susan Gordon

My Dad died December 8th, 1961

I was 14 years old.

A few days after my Dad's funeral, my Grandpa took me for a walk around the block. I can still remember my warm hand in his paper-crisp one.

"Susan," he said, "you have got to be a good girl, now."

He knew of the battles between my mother and me.

"Be a good girl, now."

I couldn't.

It was a Sunday afternoon when my mother stormed in the room.

It was not the Sunday when she pulled all of the clothes out of messy closets and threw them on the floor.

Roar

It was a warm, clear Sunday, when she came into my room and said, "If you don't get your French grade up, I am going to give your dog away."

She didn't say "Buttons" the name of my little salt and pepper schnauzer, "Buttons," that my Dad had bought for me.

No, it was just my mother in a Sunday tizzy, after church, trying to get me to straighten up before she walked out the door to her new job.

When my Dad had died, he left Mom with four of us. I was 14; Diane was 10, John was 6 and Bruce had just turned 2. And Dad left my mother with a mortgage and Grandpa to take care of.

Mom had started to work for Russell T. Baker Realty at the end of January because her friend from church, AE Hurt, also a realtor, had said, "Doris, I think you could do this job."

And real estate – it sounds easy, doesn't it? It sounds part time. But it is neither if you are trying to support a family on the money you make when you only make a sale. It is all commissions, no salary.

I have a memory from that winter of my mother sitting at her small, dark desk counting up the money she had to feed us and pay the mortgage. I remember a total of 489.00 dollars.

She thought of quitting and going to work as a secretary, although that wouldn't have fed us either.

But Tim Baker could see how good my mother would be and he said, "Doris, I'll stake you." That was in February and by July my Mom was selling houses. She was 41 when my Dad died, and by the time she was 44, she was the best salesperson in Baltimore County. It was a man's game back then and there she was. She would sell real estate for the next 38 years and she was never out of the top three. I have a picture of Mom from those days. She is tiny, 5'1"; her red hair is curled back in those soft 1960's waves and cut to the nape of her neck. She is dressed in a light turquoise Jackie Kennedy A-line dress with a high jeweled collar. She is standing between Vince Gallow, 6'3", sales manager and her brother, Bob, who tops out at 5'7". The two men are holding a check that says one million dollars; that's how many houses, a million dollars' worth of houses, that my Mom had sold some time in the 1960s.

But, we didn't know that back then.

Who knows what set her off that Sunday?

My failing grades for sure; maybe she was worried about whether Grandpa and I would watch the other kids;

maybe she was worried about getting the new listing or filling the open house.

I don't know the answer. I just remember her standing in the doorway of the bedroom, the bedroom she and Dad had made for Diane and me.

Mom had bought blue polished cotton with little white sprigs and red berries on it. She had made bedspreads, one for my bed, one for Diane's and taken the rest of the material and made curtains for all three windows. Dad had taken the short end of that room and made a long white Formica desk that ran from side to side. It was 1959 and Formica was brand new back then. Then he built a chest of drawers for beneath the desk, leaving a place for me to sit and one for Diane. He built bookcases above the desks, one for each of us.

The two of them were so proud of this first bought single family house, a red brick Dutch Colonial. They were able to buy it cheap because it was painted battleship grey, floors, ceilings and walls. But my Mom and Dad were a team and this house was something they could tackle. I still remember my Mom with turquoise paint in her red hair from painting the inside of kitchen cabinets.

What they hadn't planned on was my Dad's heart beginning to give way.

It was 1960. There were no bypasses back then, no stents. The doctors just said, "Dr. Kessler, stop smoking, put that pipe away; no more cheese, no more eggs, no more whole milk, no more red meat." My Dad did all of that and I expect there were Presbyterian prayers, but I don't know how they could have done any good because if you are Presbyterian everything is pre-ordained. My Dad died a few weeks after my youngest brother, Bruce, turned two.

My Dad had died, the person who was always a buffer between Mom and me, and now we were left, stark-naked, with each other.

Mom was spitting words at me. "Get that French grade up."

It never occurred to me that we were both grief-crazed.

I just knew there was no way I could get that French grade up – so I left.

And if you are wondering about the plan a 14-year-old could devise, here was mine.

Buttons and I would walk north through Baltimore County, hang a right and walk north into Harford County, 40 miles all told. I would find the lady who bred Buttons and I would go to work in her kennel, earning Buttons' and my keep.

That plan had a few holes. I didn't know that lady's name; I didn't know where she lived; I didn't have an address. I just remembered that she lived in a pitched-roofed, dark green house at the end of a long lane with hemlocks on one side, kennels outside the house and puppies in the kitchen.

And knowing just that and not one whit more, I clipped the leash on Buttons' collar and set out. Now, Buttons might not have come with me if she had known how little I knew. I walked up Carolina Road, across Chesapeake Ave, into Towson proper, up Bosley, down Bosley and out onto Delaney Valley Road.

I was walking the same route we used to take for Sunday drives when my Dad was still alive, out Delaney Valley Road, out to Loch Raven Reservoir. My Mom loved these Sundays because she wasn't in charge; Dad was. John, Diane and I would be piled into the back seat and Bruce would be up front with Mom and Dad. And Dad would be singing: "I've been working on the railroad all the live long day; I've been working on the railroad just to pass the time away. Can't you hear the whistle blowing? Rise up so early in the morn. Can't you hear the Captain calling, 'Dinah blow your horn?'" Or he could have been singing: "She'll Be Coming Round the Mountain," or my favorite, "Swing Low Sweet Chariot." Dad would drive around the reservoir, cross the bridge and we would always park and walk down beneath those tall pines, down to the water. If it was summer, we'd take our shoes off and wade in the reservoir even though it was our drinking water.

And then, back in the car, Dad would take a right hand turn on a macadam road to Cloverland Dairy Farms, the farm with the Golden Guernsey cows, the cows that gave our milk. The dairy farm had a big show barn. When you walked in, one whole side was glass and if it was milking time, one prize Golden Guernsey cow after another would be led in and attached to the milking machine and her white milk would go sluicing through a glass pipe. And if you turned away from the cows the whole other side of the barn was low wooden stalls filled with fragrant, clean straw and in each of those stalls was a Golden Guernsey calf. When you reached in to stroke its head, its long pink tongue would come out and suck in your jacket sleeve. Once we'd finished petting the calves, we walked out of the show barn and into a low concrete building where they made ice cream. My mother's favorite was butter pecan.

I don't know how many hours had passed; I'd left the house when the sun was directly overhead. Now it was much lower in the sky.

Buttons and I surely walked five miles.

We probably walked eight.

We made it to the bridge that crossed the reservoir.

Roar

But by then we were bleeding.

I can't remember if it was her or me.

It might have been her paws or my nose.

I remember sitting on the side of the road in the late afternoon sun thinking: "I can't make it."

It was a wave that nearly drowned me.

Somehow, I turned back, took the right-hand fork for Cloverland Farms.

When I got there, I asked to use their phone. I don't know who I called. I don't know who came out to get me. I don't remember anything my mother said to me though we were both there when the dark took the house.

I just remember my ten-year-old sister, Diane, catching me by the kitchen door, and hissing at me, "Did you forget it was Mother's Day?"

Two Blocks from Home

Courtney Crane

I headed out the door with Elnora's grocery list scratched in pencil on the back of Mom's thank-you note from Aunt Lummy. I told Elnora it would be ok to write her list on the back of the note, even if it was on monogrammed paper, it was already stained with a coffee cup ring. I liked when Elnora sent me to Piggly Wiggly. Mom never did. Mom called me the "absent-minded professor", and babied me even though I was almost twelve and a half. But Elnora gave me little jobs after school. We polished silver together and ate Frito and bologna sandwiches smothered in her homemade mayonnaise, the color of puss. She was often in a last-minute rush planning our dinner and would send me to pick up kidney beans or butter and sometimes her Pall Mall Menthols too. I just charged it all on our Piggly Wiggly account, plus they knew me there, so I just brought my house key clipped to my belt loop with a carabiner I got at camp.

Walking past Dominican College, I admired the cool college girls huddled on white benches in the courtyard, studying and smoking cigarettes. The tall white Virgin Mary statue hovered over them with her out stretched arms and downcast expression. That stone faced Virgin Mary always gave me the creeps.

I crossed St. Charles Avenue and walked one more block to Piggly Wiggly. Elnora's list on the monogrammed paper was folded up and sweaty in my palm. I said "Hi" to old Mr. Gautreaux hunched behind the counter with his crossword puzzle, and went back to the chilly meat section to see the cow tongues. Ever since I was little, I was drawn to the thick cow tongues on styrofoam trays wrapped tight in plastic. When the butcher wasn't looking, I'd press my palm over the wrapped meat, feeling the bumpy taste buds through the plastic. I used to have nightmares thinking about those dumb eyed cows sprawled in spreading pools of blood, their throats slashed and tongues cut out by rednecked farmers. The bloody back story of the cow tongues fed my dark imagination more than the regular old meat like flank steak or chicken breasts.

My stomach was growling and I couldn't wait for beef stew tonight for dinner. It was my favorite, except for the slimy okra chunks I'd pick out and ball up in a napkin. Elnora's grocery list was long today. The bell peppers, beef chuck, potatoes and all were a tight fit in one doubled up paper bag. I held the bag close on my right hip, the same way I held my baby cousin Janie, and crossed back over St. Charles avenue, past Dominican College towards home. The benches where the college girls had been sitting were empty. A black crow perched on the Virgin Mary statue's pious head, peering down at me as I took a short cut home through the campus, to the shady side street draped in willows.

A beat-up Oldsmobile rumbled toward me. I saw a pasty bearded man behind the wheel with his elbow hanging out the window. He smiled as he pulled over and asked me directions to Tulane University. Opening the passenger door, he patted the stained seat beside him, and said, "Why don't you sit down a minute?" He had a raspy, cowboy voice, long brown Jesus hair and a dark beard. His black button down shirt was pulled tight across his belly, untucked over faded jeans and tennis shoes. He wasn't wearing a seat belt. Without thinking, I just slid into the front seat next to him, while giving directions to Tulane, "Take a right at the light, go straight down St. Charles Avenue to Broadway and turn left…" I held the Piggly Wiggly bag on my lap. I knew Elnora needed me to get back with the groceries so she could make dinner before Mom returned from the Junior League and dad got off the downtown streetcar. Elnora had told me "no dawdlin' today," but here I sat in a car with this strange man, two blocks from home.

He wasn't even writing down the directions to Tulane. He just nodded "uh huh" and wrapped his arm around my shoulders. He smelled like B.O. and woodsy cologne. Deep lines like cracked clay surrounded his blood shot blue eyes. I think they were blue eyes, I don't really know. I only glanced at his face then turned away. His breath was warm. My cheeks turned red. I gripped the grocery bag. The man must've thought I was such a baby, with my light blue corduroys, and checked collar popping out of my Country Day school sweatshirt. With one hand around my shoulder, he ran his other grubby hand on top of the red and blue C.D. block letters over my boobs. My chest stiffened as I arched my back towards him…He did all this in the afternoon light on Pine Street, and I let him. I had never even kissed a boy, much less all this. I felt heat between my legs – heat mixed with nausea. I was shaking as he kissed my brown hair and neck. I stared straight ahead, hoping I wouldn't vomit into the Piggly Wiggly bag. He grabbed the bag with one hand and placed it by my feet. He had dirty fingernails.

He said how pretty I was and how I should be a model and he knew an agency across the lake, and he could tell them about me. He never asked me my name. I didn't ask his. I didn't say a word. Licking my chapped lips, I just looked straight ahead and hoped he wouldn't try to kiss my mouth. What if I had bad breath or food caught in my braces? He moved his hand under my shirt and fiddled with my white cotton training bra. He gave up trying to unhook it, reached under and pinched my hard nipple between his fingers. Without looking down, I felt his thing pressed hard on my thigh like a hot sweet potato, about to burst from his jeans. My breath was short. He swiped his long Jesus hair out of his eyes and glanced out the open car windows, before putting his head under my shirt. As he kissed my stomach, I held it in and wondered if he thought I was fat.

Mom said I wasn't fat, but needed "to watch it". She kept her weight at 119 pounds, just like Jackie Kennedy did. I tried her diet of creole tomatoes, cottage cheese and black coffee, but just couldn't do it. Elnora hugged me tight and said how I didn't need to be some "skinny minnie" like mom and Jackie Kennedy, and that most boys like girls with "meat on their bones".

I sucked my stomach in tighter while the man patted my shoulder and told me to relax. We were both breathing hard...I hoped the dampness I felt wasn't leaky period blood. I had never had this heavy, wet, buzzy feeling in "my privates". The man looked out the car window again before unzipping my corduroys. My faded underwear with hearts and worn elastic peaked out. I didn't want him to see this babyish underwear from 5th grade, that I saved in the back of the drawer for my period week. Plus, I had a big maxi pad jammed in there and would die if he saw that. In a high-pitched voice I said, "Wait...wait... stop...get off me, I have my period". With a fist full of his long hair, I yanked the man's head up from my lap, grabbed my bag, opened the door and stumbled away from the car, as the bell peppers rolled onto the curb. I heard the man yell after me, "Remember, I really can get you that modeling job." Adjusting my zipper with one hand, I held the ripped bag with the other, and ran towards home on shaky legs. I heard the Oldsmobile rumble away and didn't look back.

I told Elnora I was late because I ran into a school friend and that I forgot the bell peppers. But I never told her or anyone else what I did that day on the way back from Piggly Wiggly. I didn't know at the time how lucky I was to still be alive, that the man didn't drive off with me tied up in the trunk, or cut my tongue out like those poor cows. At night in bed I closed my eyes tight and tried to wish away the shame from that day, the way Elnora used to close her eyes, and hold my pinky toe to "wish away" the warts I got at camp…That's how I thought about it for my first fifty years – as something I did, that was my fault, not as something that happened to twelve-year-old me, two blocks from home. I never walked to Piggly Wiggly alone again.

Don't Tell My Husband I'm Lonely

Sheila Grinell

My husband was diagnosed with Parkinson's disease in 2011. I had noticed the first sign of his decline six years earlier: he dragged his bare feet across the tile floor of the bathroom, making a sloppy, floppy sound that got on my nerves. When I protested, he seemed oblivious. I learned to avoid being barefoot together in the bathroom.

Tom had had an "essential tremor" – his right hand shook for no obvious cause – for decades. In 2008, though, he noticed that other things weren't right, and it was affecting his driving. So, we went to a neurologist, who sent us to a neuropsychologist to assess Tom's mental capacity. Diagnosis: "mild cognitive impairment," which means your mental functioning is not quite up to age-adjusted norms, but your daily life can proceed. Tom was 70 at the time. He went back to work, and I went about my business.

Three years passed. One day, Tom found himself in his car in the middle of an intersection near our home, at a complete loss as to what to do next. He got scared. Back we went to the neurologist, who looked at him and said,

"You have Parkinson's." Then I got online. We read. We talked to people in the know. We signed him up for classes at the Muhammad Ali Parkinson's Center here in Phoenix.

Life began to change.

I had to drive Tom to classes at the Center because he couldn't negotiate the highway safely. Ten months later, he quit his job. I took over management of his daily activities because he couldn't read the calendar anymore. When he looked at a page, the markings didn't mean anything – he couldn't identify a specific activity without my guidance. This was a man, my man, who began his working life at IBM fixing machines.

Most people think of Parkinson's as a movement disorder; they visualize Michael J. Fox bouncing around when he talks. Yes, "PD" affects movement, but it affects everything else, too: automatic processes like digestion and swallowing, cognitive processes like planning and spatial orientation, and emotional processes like mood and dreams. In PD, neurons in a particular part of the brain die in a particular way, and the available amount of the brain signaling chemical dopamine is diminished. With a weaker signal, it's harder to turn circuits on. A PD sufferer has to push hard to compensate; he has to feel like he's shouting in order to raise his voice above a whisper. PD is progressive and incurable. A medicine that restores dopamine to the brain helps most patients – until too many neurons have died for the drug to make a significant difference.

Tom's biggest deficits are cognitive, not motor or emotional. When we watch a movie together, I have to pause every so often to explain the plot twists. He hates needing help, but he's glad when the movie starts to make more sense. Odd, unpredictable things happen in his brain: once he hit the switch to close the garage door just before I backed out (he thought he was opening the door, although it was already open). That misconception cost $1900 for a new door, not to mention the psychic wear and tear. (Why didn't he check? Why didn't I double-check?)

Sometimes our day feels like business as usual: I buy food and cook; we eat and he washes up – he leaves blotches here and there, which I remove later – and we both tend to the dog. Then I notice that he's asking the same question twice, maybe three times. When I call him on it, he says he can't remember what I've said. But there's nothing wrong with his memory (it's been tested). You can't remember what you haven't registered in the first place.

Why, you ask, do I call him on it? He can't help not being able to focus. Yet I react instinctively, feeling that surely, if he tried hard enough, he could pay better attention – to me, his constant support, the one who ensures he takes his medicine on time and calls the Uber driver when required. I deserve all the effort he can muster! Then I ask myself, is it reasonable to expect him to make an extra effort all day long? I cool off, and I get contrite. I say nothing, he says nothing. We resume business as usual.

The hard part comes at bedtime, when I start to talk about little things that have populated my day, or big things that loom ahead, and I see Tom's not following. I take a breath and start again, laying it out slowly, carefully, and sometimes he responds with the empathy and people smarts that I fell in love with 35 years ago. (Recently, a neighbor asked us to his wedding. Tom said to me, "I sense he wants us to say no." Sure enough, the promised invitation didn't arrive.) But often I can't get through. He looks at me, puzzled, as if I'm telling a joke and he's waiting for the punch line, which doesn't come. He's not the companion he once was. I sorely miss that man. Without him, I'm lonely.

A friend whose husband died young from a brain wasting disorder told me she used to ask herself what percentage of time her husband was a helpmate versus a dependent. Right now, Tom is fifty-fifty. He is so unsure of himself that he checks in with me constantly, rechecking things he knows, like when the PBS Newshour starts, "just to be sure." He walks three steps behind me in airports and department stores so he won't worry about getting lost.

We still love each other; we still share values and sympathies (not to mention children and grandchildren). But there's less substance to our marriage than before. We can't go on physical or imaginative journeys together. Everything we can do together takes so much more time.

A little while ago, after someone prodded me, I realized my discomfort goes deeper than day-to-day frustration. At bottom lies the knowledge that I have lost the future I once assumed I'd have. I have lost the freedom to plan the last decades of my life. I grieve that loss, not actively, but steadily. My grief is like the buzz of a fluorescent light, always in the background although mostly ignored. Each time PD steals something new from me – Tom just gave up "happy hour" because he can't keep up with the conversation (he had already given up drink) – I grieve a little more.

I know I'm not alone. Women everywhere are caring for someone with damaged cognition. Far more women than men wind up in charge of a declining parent or spouse. Most of the time, they shoulder the burden willingly. But it takes a toll. More than 60% of caregivers die before their demented relatives do. (I've asked Tom what would happen if I died first. He said, "I'll survive." He doesn't really appreciate the level of organization that would be required.)

I have two remedies for what ails me. First, I retreat from my husband's needs for a few hours every day when I sit behind my computer, writing. Tom sometimes pokes his head into my office and asks, "Are you still at the machine?" He'd rather have my company, but he knows I need to do what I do – to engage with my whole self in the wider world, without him. Right now, he can handle the closed office door, and he's proud of my accomplishments. As he continues to decline, I hope I continue to feel good about ignoring him for two hours at a clip.

And then there's my second remedy, a support group of PD spouses, twelve women and four men, that meets once a month. No matter what I blurt, everyone "gets it" – they've been there or are going there – and their compassion is boundless. Sometimes we exchange tips on caregiving, like how to give your loved one a shot of oxygen before a long flight to compensate for the effects of lowered air pressure. Or where to find a special kind of door hinge that makes the doorway a few inches wider so a wheelchair can pass through.

Sometimes we talk about our own needs, and then, for once, we take center-stage, not the disease wasting our partners. We say things we wouldn't dare say to our adult children when they ask how it's going. A few of us have begun to meet for lunch, sharing our dreams and cheering each other on. These wonderful new friends will be with me for the long haul. I cherish them. They keep loneliness at bay.

Roar

Rising Above the Unconscionable

Daya Wakens

It was peculiar he wore a gun on his hip and he was not in law enforcement. On our first dinner date, Tom wanted to know everything about me. He bragged about himself and his cousin, a State Trooper. He was average looking, but his dark green eyes against his olive skin captivated me. He grew up in the same area of Rochester, NY, as me, yet none of my friends had heard of him. They viewed him as arrogant, unsocial, and not good enough for me. I ignored their opinions with hope they would see what I saw. I was a single mother in my early twenties and he was ten years my senior, but had no children. Tom contacted me each day and within three months, I was swept into an exclusive relationship showered in compliments.

My son, Jeremy, was two years old with a head full of brown curls and wide brown eyes. He was the center of my universe and Tom adored him. I told Tom I wanted to complete my college degree at night school so I could get a higher paying job. He was proud of his construction job. In the late '70s, jobs were plentiful, but I needed a college degree to earn near his paycheck and not have to depend on Planned Parenthood to provide my female healthcare. He said he would be supportive of me and we were meant to be together as a family. I married into his huge family.

About a year after our marriage, everything changed. Tom began boasting about his family and degrading my siblings and friends. I was mortified. His family spoke of "Jew bastards, queers that are sinners, and the N-word" at the holiday dinner table. I asked, "What if one of them saved your life one day?" All the men cocked their eyebrows and the women looked down at the table. At home, I asked Tom not to use racial slurs, especially in front of my son. I'd meet up with my sister in secrecy until the day he found us in a restaurant, threw me over his shoulder and carried me out yelling "You are my wife, you belong home." He was always right. I suffered his relentless wrath with sleepless nights until I'd agree with him. To avoid his endless rants, I honored his wishes.

After he hounded me, I obtained my pistol permit. He was more excited to teach me how to use a gun than I was. At community service events, he sat me close enough to see him accept his awards, but far from conversations. Compliments from strangers were plenty, but no longer from him. His charm secured his "Perfect Husband" image as he positioned me into perpetual chaos.

We both worked. In addition, I attended night school in an eighteen-month college program. One Saturday morning, I awoke later than usual and Tom surprised me with a dozen long-stem red roses. It filled my heart, until I got into the shower.

"Why is my vagina shaved? Why are my breasts bruised?"

"It was sexually exciting for me."

"Wait a minute. I have no memory of it!"

"You slept through it."

"What?"

"You were tired. Maria, I didn't think you would be upset."

I could not understand how I could "sleep" through the things he did to me. He ignored my confusion and promised to never do anything to my body without my consent. I forgave him as a good Catholic wife, but a piece of me had been stripped away.

I completed my degree and within two months of my new dream job, Tom demanded I quit. He feared others would think he was not a good provider. I refused and the "stubborn son-of-a-bitches" he flung at me eventually stopped hurting. We moved into our new house with the white picket fence wrapped around the backyard with plenty of space for our doghouse, garden, and swimming pool. He refused to help me install floor tiles in four rooms, but quickly accepted compliments as if he installed the floors. I provided home-cooked meals, an impeccably clean house, and crisp clean clothes, yet nothing was good enough.

I enjoyed watching Jeremy's Little League baseball games, but Tom always had an excuse to stay home. He never joined our bicycle rides, toboggan trips, or vacations either. I wanted a sibling for Jeremy, but Tom refused to get tested and blamed me for not conceiving a child. Our lovemaking swung from sensual to him violently hammering me with his empty stare until my cries of pain relieved him. It was as if I was an object, and not human. He assured me he would try to be gentle, but I had to keep reminding him.

A couple years into our marriage, I accidently found a packet of twenty-four photos in his dresser drawer, developed clear across the country nine months prior. The first few were naked areas of a female body with bruises taken at various angles on an unfamiliar bedspread. The eighth photo knocked me to my knees. I would have never known my uterus could have been vacuumed out with the head of a beer bottle or my vagina could have been filled with broken glass. Handcuffed to our bed, my eyes were swollen shut and my body was completely lifeless. It was a sadistic rape session. I still have no memory of the staged event and only the horrendous evidence that described every detail. Mysterious bruises over the years finally made sense.

Distraught, my sister and I brought the photos to his cousin, the State Trooper. His wife laughed and said that was something her husband would do. He flipped through the photos and looked down on the table.

"You look drunk in these pictures."

"Everyone knows I don't drink alcohol! He drugged and raped me!"

"Maybe if you spent more time with him, this would not have happened."

"He is not deprived, and even if he was, it does not entitle him to do this to me! Not long ago, he shaved my vagina as I slept and I have no memory of that. He has a serious psychological issue!"

"This is a personal issue that you both should work through."

Tom arrived, and again he displayed entitlement. I wanted to call the police department, but his cousin said we were a married couple and there are no rape charges. It was the early '80s and the truth of that magnified my pain. Tom and his cousin told me I was being irrational. I demanded he move out immediately. He agreed to separate and he moved in with his mother.

Overwhelmed in grief, I yearned for the happiness I had when I said, "I do." Tom told his family we separated because I was being irrational. Those unaware of the truth fed him sympathy. Others that knew the truth hit me with, "He's your husband and loves you. What about Jeremy? Your family belongs together…in sickness and in health." I wasn't submissive like the other wives. What was wrong with me? After three months, my family physician diagnosed my distorted spine as meningitis, but the orthopedic specialist at the hospital emergency room determined it was multiple spasms due to extreme stress in my life. I was given a three-week sick leave note and advised to relax, but I suffered a spasm next to my heart weeks later. Who will take care of Jeremy if I die? During that year of separation, Jeremy cried each day and Tom begged to come home with a promise to attend therapy sessions. I convinced myself he already did the worst to me and for Jeremy's sake, I gave him another chance. I believed his good behavior would last with therapy.

He came home with an armed security guard uniform and announced his weekend job at a warehouse. He loved coming home in uniform with free banana pies from the bakery. Jeremy was terrified when Tom flashed a fake police badge and pulled over a vehicle that passed him. He started taking nightly rides as we slept and items appeared in our basement. He labeled me "stupid" for not believing he took only things left at the curb of the warehouse. If only I would not question him, I would be perfect.

One night, about nine months after he started his weekend security job, I awoke 3 a.m. to a knock at the door. Tom was not in bed. It was his cousin, the Trooper, in uniform. Tom was in jail, charged with burglarizing the warehouse he was hired to secure.

"Tom said you would not let him buy a security baton. You need to go downtown and bail him out of jail."

"He never mentioned that to me, besides he has two. I never saw his paychecks from his security job. I refuse to go to the police station."

His cousin not only bailed Tom out of jail, he provided him a cover-up and helped him obtain another security side job. Tom handed me, "I made a mistake. Couples that love each other forgive." I asked for proof of his therapy sessions. There was none. I requested a legal separation. He refused, headed out the door, and returned with another dozen long-stem red roses. My nightmares and nighttime grinding were unstoppable. I could no longer graciously accept compliments from others.

My niece from Michigan wanted to visit for two weeks. Jeremy was excited to see his cousin and I thought it would be a good breather for me, so I agreed. Lisa bloomed into a beautiful tween full of life and Jeremy's friends loved her. At our dinner table, Tom repeatedly interrupted Jeremy and commanded her attention.

The following week after Tom left for work, Lisa came to me with tears flowing down her face. As she spoke, the walls were closing in as she led me to a neatly drilled hole in the guest bedroom wall. She saw Tom's eyeball as she undressed the night before. The hole on the other side had dust below it. I fought to push my buried pain back down inside me as I struggled to get a grip. Tom's cousin arrived in uniform and took Lisa in a room to question her before he inspected the wall. He then puked out, "Well, the good news is, this is only voyeurism, and it's nothing that can't be handled in family therapy," and followed my upset with, "There is no law against voyeurism." When Tom arrived, he denied drilling the hole in the wall and called Lisa a liar.

I yelled, "I painted this house last year and there were no holes in any of the walls! She saw your eyeball!!"

His jaw dropped and his cousin immediately whispered in his ear. Tom went into the garage and returned with supplies. They went upstairs and patched the evidence. I demanded he move out of our home immediately and screamed at his cousin, "Why do you continue to cover-up for him?" He glared at me before they headed out the door. We separated again.

My sister took the next flight to be here. At a counseling facility, Jeremy and Lisa stated that Tom did not touch them inappropriately. He stated the same and denied all guilt. He painted himself as a hard-working, stand-up citizen that fathered my son all those years. Flooded in tears, my sister and I stopped each other from killing him. She and Lisa flew home. I knew it was necessary for Tom to admit his guilt to her. Why did he do this? What if it escalated?

When Tom delivered me another dozen red roses and a religious wooden box filled with baseball cards for Jeremy, it shot me into retribution.

"You traumatized my niece! She is just a child!! I want to kill you, but I can't. Because of you, I no longer trust anyone with my son. You must admit your guilt to Lisa so she can heal!"

"Maria, I love you. This is all her fault! She made that story up. She needs counseling."

"Shoot this sick bastard" echoed, but my love for my son stopped me and led me to a counselor for strength. "I understand you forgave your husband for what he did to you to keep your family together. Some children are raped by their biological father. Many families have dysfunction and it all depends on what you are willing to work towards keeping the family together." I could not wrap my head around that and left with weakened hope.

Tom's long weeks of denial wore on me. When I voiced my urge to shoot Tom with his own gun, he finally admitted his guilt to Lisa, but his cousin helped him slip through the fingers of the law. At the counseling facility, Tom admitted he drilled the hole, but did not admit his intent and denied sexual gratification. No voyeurism law existed and no criminal charges were filed. He was only referred to a psychiatrist.

Jeremy did not want to leave his home and neighborhood he loved. Tom offered to buy me a pair of boxing gloves in lieu of punishment. A vivid memory surfaced.

"Remember years ago, I told you that if anyone sexually traumatized my son, I would kill them, and you told me that I wouldn't have to because you would do it for me? So now what? You sexually traumatized my niece. Is suicide appropriate?"

"I am doing what I can to fix this. I love you and I want my family back."

While Tom and I continued to live separately, Tom visited a psychiatrist for a year before switching to a clinical therapist that was also a Reverend. Nine months later, I was asked to join his session. When asked about my feelings, I gushed like a raging river. He gave me a moment to compose myself before his response took a layer of my skin off.

"Your husband has difficulties with his needs. He viewed your niece as a woman, and not as a child."

"WHAT?! I don't understand what you just said."

"I am explaining to you where your husband's mind was at. This is prevalent in many families and forgiveness is essential. He loves you and wants his family back, so I would like to work with you on that."

"HE DRUGGED AND RAPED ME, TWICE THAT I KNOW OF, THEN HE SEXUALLY VIOLATED MY NIECE AND TRAUMATIZED HER, AND YOUR ONLY CONCERN IS GETTING HIS FAMILY BACK TO HIM?"

"Maria, please calm down. Tom wants his family back and I would like to work on that with you."

I glared at him and heaved, "You are both warped!" I left and my sleepless nights wore on me as I dwindled down to skin and bones.

Six months later, Tom believed redemption should be granted. He demanded to move back home. Two law offices confirmed I could not stop him because both our names were on the deed. The New York State divorce law required grounds at that time and because there were no criminal charges, there was no guarantee of the outcome. He not only took my hand in marriage, he took everything inside of me.

I went to a Catholic school, was an honor student, and loved by many. Saturated in tears, I screamed, "God, why is this happening to me? Can you hear me?" I wept hysterically as visions of me relaxed six feet under the ground flashed repeatedly. Suddenly, childhood memories when I felt the safest filled me, especially Ave Maria song in Latin at Sunday Mass. While mesmerized, a surreal infusion throughout my body had followed and I emerged with resilience written across my face, unlike my childhood dream to become a ballerina. I was reminded of my belief in God and I no longer felt alone. I embraced my renewed strength. With my pastels drenched in tears, I swatted forgiveness out of my path. Buried memories unleashed and scrutiny prevailed. Was the vagina shaving preparation for the sadistic porn session he did to me, or was it preparation to fulfill a pedophilia fantasy? What else am I not aware of?

I searched the house. Multiple VHS tapes of child porn were cleverly hidden in our TV room, binoculars were stuffed in his recliner, and two taped boxes in a bedroom closet contained seventy 9mm reels of porn dated four decades prior along with a vintage projector. "Was he entertaining himself with porn when we were on the baseball field?" I recalled his mother's words. Her husband was an abusive alcoholic. He used to come home from work, grab his beer, and take Tommy upstairs to watch movies in his bed. Was it porn? Tom was five when his dad died. There was a latch hook on her bathroom door with a one-inch viewing space. She told me Tom nailed it on for her. It sickened me when she said, "Honey, you are a married woman; you need to let it go and forgive Tommy." She took her secrets to her grave.

I choked down the tangled emotions nestled in my throat and rewound to the beginning of my hell. With a list of his behavior history, including everything he made me forget, I delved into the arena of personality disorders and many character traits of antisocial personality disorder, narcissism and sociopathy. I reflected on Tom's behavior. His false charm, craving for power and admiration, manipulations, deceitfulness, pathological lies, and victim blaming helped me to understand the brainwashing process. His priority was preserving his image and exposure of his truth guaranteed punishment. The lack of a conscience, empathy, remorse, and guilt hit me hard. When I stumbled upon sadism, it triggered dry heaves. One gains gratification by sexually assaulting, humiliating, and degrading the victim. A need to be superior by violating others, without regard to human life, had slapped me in the face. I felt like an object, not human much less a wife. Were my missing worn panties over the years, trophies? Why didn't my counselor or Tom's clinical therapist mention any of this to me? Temptation to unzip my body, peel the outer layer off, and strut away was nearly overpowering.

The next evening as Tom visited Jeremy, I turned on his CB unit in his truck. I heard a woman ending a telephone conversation, and then the shower water running. She was unaware he listened to her every move in her own home. When I confronted Tom, he told me all men watch porn and swore he only listened to emergency calls on his CB unit. He told me I was overreacting and called me "crazy." I demanded a divorce. He chased me, slammed me up against the wall, and choked me until he confiscated my checkbook. "This is all her fault! I will kill you before I give you a divorce!" There was a loud knock at the front door. Tom rushed and opened the door with a smile and his signature charm. It was two State Troopers and when Tom mentioned his cousin to the State Troopers, they still filed a domestic violence report and took possession of his six handguns. I was advised to get an Order of Protection, but knew it was no guarantee. Knowing only my pistol permit could retrieve his guns, it leveled his rage.

He requested we remain married with separate lives, but I refused. He finally agreed to a legal separation.

Against advice, I let him have our house, the majority of our assets, and the privilege of telling others I destroyed our eighteen-year marriage. Our safety and my son's future was my priority, nothing else mattered. Jeremy was in his second year of college. I vomited the truth to my long-lost friends and was grateful for their love and support. Knowledge evoked the courage to shed layers of unwanted skin and move forward.

Before I pulled the truck out of the driveway, I rolled the window down.

"Your pistols are sitting next to your porn collection you stashed on the garage rafters."

"Who do you think you are?"

"Who do I think I am?

I am a human being.

I am a woman.

I am a mother."

I took back what belonged to me, myself. We moved into a highly-secured apartment and the first night I slept with both eyes closed was priceless. After two years of working overtime, Jeremy was happy with our new house and his neighborhood. I focused on Jeremy and his future along with rebuilding myself with unwavering healthy boundaries. When I was told Tom's personal computer was infested with child porn websites, I was not shocked. Tom told Jeremy that I ruined our marriage and attempted to turn my own son against me. Eventually, Jeremy distanced himself from Tom. Seven years later, Tom's clinical therapist, the Reverend, was in the media. He was accused of "an emotional relationship that was inappropriate" with a young female that was his niece through marriage. I learned a perpetrator will defend another of the same. Tom called and spoke to me as if we were still a married couple for a few years. I longed for the eyes behind my head to disappear and for the day I would no longer have to sleep with my loaded gun nearby.

Between 1984 and 2003, the marital rape and porn laws United States enacted could have put Tom behind bars for quite some time. The voyeurism law enacted states it is only a crime if it is recorded. The "Statute of Limitations" continues to protect sexual predators, only a handful of states do not. Worse yet, we have good women behind bars for doing what was necessary to protect herself and her children from this inhumane barbaric treatment. What will it take to change cultural mindsets?

By 2017, sexual assault has been given the public recognition it deserves, especially campus date rape, but our sexual assault laws still need improvement. In the meantime, I only have the promise I made to myself after Tom was out of my life. My grandchildren will be taught to respect all humanity and the clear definition of sexual assault much sooner than the "Birds and the Bees" talk. Whether my granddaughters choose to wear pastel dresses and high heels, or not, they will be empowered and will have to learn how to fight like a man to protect themselves. I am what emerged from my journey of love, compassion, empathy, and sorrow!

Eventually my soulmate entered my life. He gave me a dozen long-stem red roses only once, but never again. He understands my past, my present, and stands strong beside me. He became my best friend and my husband. My morals and values along with my belief in God had fueled my fire that gave me the strength to believe in myself and rise above. I own every stretch mark, scar, and earned stripe on my body. I am proud to be a woman.

Roar

My Abortion, at 23 Weeks

Judy Nicastro

I believe that parenthood starts before conception, at the moment you decide you want a child, and are ready and able to create a safe and loving home for her or him. I support abortion rights, but I reject the false distinction between the terms "pro-choice" and "pro-life." Here's why.

A lawyer by training, I was 38 when I completed a term on the Seattle City Council. Two years later, I married my husband, who is five years younger. We wanted children, and started trying right away, but had trouble conceiving.

Using in vitro fertilization, we had our son, Matthew, now 4. When he was 2, after another round of I.V.F., we conceived again. I was six weeks pregnant when I learned I was carrying twins, a boy and a girl. We were elated.

But in my 20th week, during an ultrasound, the technician looked concerned, and we got the first hint that something might be wrong. The next day, a Friday, my obstetrician called to say that the technician had had a hard time seeing the heart of the male fetus. "It is probably just the position," she reassured me. I wasn't reassured.

On Monday, I had a second ultrasound and my husband and I spent two hours – it felt like an eternity – with a different doctor and technician. "It looks as if the boy has a herniated diaphragm," they told us. "All the organs are in his chest and not developing."

I began sobbing. What did that mean? Would the organs move? Was my baby "fixable"? The clinic staff members were reluctant to tell us how bad it was. They said I needed an M.R.I., which would provide more details.

My world stopped. I loved being pregnant with twins and trying to figure out which one was where in my uterus. Sometimes it felt like a party in there, with eight limbs moving. The thought of losing one child was unbearable.

The M.R.I., at Seattle Children's Hospital, confirmed our fears: the organs were pushed up into our boy's chest and not developing properly. We were in the 22nd week. In Washington State, abortion is legal until the 24th week.

After 10 more days of tests and meetings, we were in the 23rd week and had to make a decision. My husband is more conservative than I am. He also is a Catholic. I am an old-school liberal, and I am not religious. But from the start, and through this ordeal, we were in complete agreement. We desperately wanted this child and would do whatever we could to save him, if his hernia was fixable and he could have a good quality of life.

Once we had all the data, we met with a nurse, a surgeon and a pediatrician at the hospital. The surgeon said our boy had a hole in his diaphragm. Only one lung chamber had formed, and it was only 20 percent complete. If our boy survived birth, he would be on oxygen and other life supports for a long time. The thought of hearing him gasp for air and linger in pain was our nightmare.

The surgeon described horrible intervention procedures that would give our son the only potential chance of surviving birth, such as before cutting the umbilical cord he would have a tube put down his throat to help him breath because he had only 20% of one lung. He would NEVER be without machines to help him breathe. We were horrified. The pediatrician could tell that we were looking for candid guidance. He cautioned that medical ethics constrained what he could say, then added, "Termination is a reasonable option, and a reasonable option that I can support." The surgeon and nurse nodded in agreement. I burst out sobbing. My husband cried, too. But in a sense, the pediatrician's words were a source of comfort and kindness. They were honest. He said, "'Sometimes we can keep people alive, but at what cost, what type of life is it?" He said what we already knew.

The next day, at a clinic near my home, I felt my son's budding life end as a doctor inserted a needle through my belly into his tiny heart. She had trouble finding it because of its abnormal position. As horrible as that moment was – it will live with me forever – I am grateful. We made sure our son was not born only to suffer. He died in a warm and loving place, inside me.

In having the abortion, we took a risk that my body would expel both fetuses, and that we would lose our daughter too. In fact, I asked if we could postpone the abortion until the third trimester, by which time my daughter would have been almost fully developed; my doctor pointed out that abortions after 24 weeks were illegal. Thankfully, Kaitlyn was born, healthy and beautiful and we love her to pieces. My little boy partially dissolved into me, and I like to think his soul is in his sister.

This horrific experience brought me to realize the fake distinction between Pro-life and Pro-choice. The Pro-life political movement is a lie. I consider myself Pro-life because I believe life means quality of life. It is anti-life and cruel to have a living being born only to suffer. I am also Pro-choice because I know from experience how important it is for every woman and who ever she decides to tell to decide what is best for her and her life.

We made the choice to terminate our baby because, legally we were able to and because, morally, it was the best choice.

I don't know if Roe v. Wade will be overturned in my lifetime, but the chipping away of abortion rights is occurring at an astounding pace. I share my story in the hope that our leaders will be more responsible and compassionate when they weigh what it means to truly value the lives of women and children.

Roar

Lucky

Mary Supley Foxworth

I splashed some cold water on my face. Feeling slightly more awake and alert, I turned my gaze from the mirror to the bathroom window. The sun was already up and shining down on the sea of row houses and apartment buildings. It looked like the start of a nice spring day, except I had no idea where I was.

The previous day, instead of one that was frightened and confused, the bathroom mirror reflected a cheerful image as I got myself ready for work. It was a Friday in April of 1997. The weekend would be here soon, and so would my friend Alec.

Alec and I had met seven years earlier. He was part of a close group of friends – mostly guys, with a shared interest in science fiction and role-playing games – who had known each other for years, with some friendships extending back to elementary school. I met Alec and the rest of them through my high school boyfriend and they all became important to me. By and large, they were my social life; that did include dating a couple of them over the years, but, I felt lucky that we all managed to maintain our friendships through the break-ups. These were the people I trusted and counted on when my father left and my family sort of fell apart, the people who listened and consoled me as I dealt with the transition to adulthood.

At 24, I was still struggling with that transition, weighed down by student loans and other financial obligations, uncertain of my career path, and lonely a lot of the time. My on-again, off-again relationship was off. My roommate was in the starry-eyed, all-consuming phase of a new romance. Most of my friends were still in school and either out of town or buried in work.

Alec was finishing up a graduate degree a few hours away, at a university in the shadow of the Blue Ridge Mountains. He was coming home to Northern Virginia for an appointment that Friday and staying at his parents' house for the weekend. I found myself looking forward to Alec's visit as I commuted to my job in DC and went about my work.

In the early afternoon, the receptionist buzzed me on my phone to let me know I had a call. I asked her to connect us and picked up the receiver to hear a familiar voice.

It was Alec. He had arrived in town.

"Are you still free tonight?" he asked. "I was thinking maybe we could go out in Adams Morgan. You could show me some of the places where you like to go out."

We made plans to meet at my apartment that evening so we could drive together in one car.

At the time, Adams Morgan was one of DC's hot spots for people in their 20s. I'd be happy to play tour guide for Alec.

After we hung up the phone, I returned my attention to my work so I could leave on time. I packed up around 5:30 and drove to my apartment in Alexandria, about 20 minutes outside of the city. I changed into a more casual outfit – khakis and a white button-down – filled the pockets of my jacket with what I'd need for the night – keys, ID, credit card, and a little cash – and then settled onto the couch to relax in front of the TV for a while. When Alec arrived, I buzzed him into the building and greeted him with a hug at my door. I introduced him to my roommate Eric and, though there wasn't much to see, I showed him around our place. Then I tossed on my jacket and we headed out.

Alec offered to drive. I had just fought my way through the crowded streets of the city a couple of hours ago, and parking in Adams Morgan was hard to come by, so I was happy to slip into the passenger seat of his car. On the way downtown, he filled me in on his semester and his job search, and I told him about the projects on which I was working and the latest goings on in my family.

It was closing in on 9 by the time Alec parked in Adams Morgan. The night air was unusually warm for that time of year, so I decided to leave my jacket in his car. I barely had room for my ID, credit card, and cash in the single pocket of my pants, so my keys stayed in my jacket pocket.

"Where should we have dinner?" Alec asked.

I was starving. I'd been so focused on work, that I didn't eat lunch and had just had a small snack at my apartment. "Let's see who has open tables."

We walked down 18th Street. It was still early for the bars and clubs, but the restaurants were packed. I was starting to wonder if we would have to head to the Golden Arches when Alec spotted a place with space. La Fourchette, a French café, had a narrow dining room and outdoor seating. The hostess led us to a table for two out on the sidewalk, along the railing that demarcated their outdoor dining area. We ordered dinner and glasses of their cheaper wine. Our entrées took a long time to arrive, but the drinks came quickly. I was tipsy by the time there was any food on my fork.

The neighborhood was really coming to life as we neared the end of dinner. People streamed by in both directions, headed to places like Cities, Millie & Al's, Tryst, Dan's Café, Crush, Heaven, Hell, and Madam's Organ. Suddenly, one of them stopped next to our table.

"A rose for the lady?"

One of the highlights of Adams Morgan, for me and many others, was the Compliment Man. He mixed with the crowds on the main streets and doled out free compliments. I loved the chance to talk with him. On the other hand, I loathed the flower sellers. They wandered in and out of the restaurants and bars, usually later in the evening, and tried to get men to buy flowers for the women around them. No matter who I was with, this intrusion always felt awkward and I'd taken to brusquely saying, "No!" and hurrying them away.

So it was with this flower seller. "No," I said, "we're not interested."

At the same time though, Alec was saying, "Yes."

"What are you doing?" I asked.

"I want to get you flowers."

"Why? No!"

Despite my continued protests that I didn't want any flowers, Alec handed over some cash to the flower seller, who handed me two red roses.

I excused myself and went to the restroom to get a little space. Alec was trying to hijack the night. He was trying to turn this into a date, when it most definitely wasn't. He'd tried something like this a few years before, giving me a card for Valentine's Day; I told him at the time that I really appreciated our friendship but didn't think anything more was a good idea. I was frustrated that it seemed I needed to reiterate that message.

When I got back to the table, I suggested we get the check. Alec had already paid it. I tried to give him money for my share, but he refused. I wasn't going to let my arm be twisted.

"I'll buy drinks at the next place then, because it's not like we're on a date." It sounded harsh to me, but I wanted to be clear.

Alec chuckled.

We got up and I left the roses on the table. Alec grabbed them.

Maybe I hadn't been clear enough. "Look, I don't want to carry those around all night. I really wish you hadn't bought them."

"I'll carry them for you," Alec replied.

"Maybe we should call it a night," I said.

"Why?"

"I thought we were going out as friends."

"Yeah, of course," Alec said.

"Really? It seems you're hoping for something else."

"Yes. Come on. Let's go to Toledo Lounge." He seemed embarrassed.

I didn't want to make him uncomfortable. I could pretend like this hadn't happened if he could.

Toledo Lounge was probably my favorite bar in Adams Morgan. It was smaller and friendlier, with less posturing than many of its competitors, and, usually, less crowded.

Not that night. It was hard to make our way to the bar. Alec ordered a beer and I got a vodka tonic and started a tab, determined to pay for our drinks. We stood in the crowd drinking and talking, though that was hard given the volume in there. As the evening wore on, a couple of seats at the bar opened up and we sat down. It wasn't long before the guy to my right leaned over to introduce himself.

"Hi, I'm Ja…"

What was that? I really couldn't hear. I asked him if he could repeat what he'd said.

"I'm Ja…"

Jason? James? I wasn't sure, but I was able to catch a hint of his British accent.

"I'm Mary," I said and shook his extended him. He then leaned over to introduce himself to Alec and offered to buy our next round of drinks.

"No, thanks," Alec replied, but James was already talking to the bartender.

The three of us shared a round of drinks – maybe my third vodka tonic of the night, I wasn't sure – and chatted, as much as that was possible over the conversations, laughter, and music that filled the bar. I was enjoying James' stories, punctuated by more drinks, but Alec wasn't interested in either. He seemed annoyed at this intrusion into our evening out. To me, meeting people was part of the fun of Adams Morgan.

I lost track of time. Alec excused himself to the restroom and James ordered vodka shots for the two of us. The shot glasses piled up on the bar in front of us until there were at least six.

When Alec returned, he said it was late and he was ready to leave. I paid the tab and stood up, unsteady on my feet from the night of drinking. James paid his tab and walked out with us.

"Where are we going next?" James asked.

"Home," Alec said.

"Let's get something to eat," James suggested.

There were a lot of places for late-night food in Adams Morgan and that sounded like a good idea to me. But Alec was adamant: he was going home.

"Alec, this will be fun," I said. He stood firm.

"C'mon on, man," James said as he put his arm around me.

We stood there on the street, the three of us. Alec and I went back and forth for several rounds of:

"I want to go out."

"I want to go home."

No amount of my drunken cajoling seemed like it was going to work.

Finally, Alec said, "You can go. I'm going home." And he turned and walked away.

James led me, stumbling a bit, in the opposite direction. I'm not sure where we ended up going for food. I wasn't feeling great from the evening of wine and vodka and excused myself to find the ladies' room. While I was in there, the zipper on my pants broke. I fumbled with it for a while in my inebriated state, but couldn't get it to budge. It was a lengthy struggle to pull my pants down and then back up without being able to unzip them. James had already ordered something at the counter by the time I rejoined him.

And then it goes dark.

I woke up the next morning in a sparsely furnished row house that was filled with light, with no idea where I was or how I got there. James was lying next to me. I was not happy that my clothes were a bit disheveled. I didn't know what James' intentions might have been, but I was never so thankful for a broken zipper.

I got out of bed without disturbing him and wandered around to find the bathroom. I expected or, at the very least, hoped to recognize something as I looked out the window. No, I didn't know if I was still in DC even. My absolute disorientation left me terrified.

I went back to the bed and woke James up. He put an arm around me and tried to land a kiss but I pulled away.

"Where are we?" I asked.

"You're at my place," he said. "You were too drunk to get home last night."

"Well, where do you live? I need to get home."

"It's too early. Come back to bed." He tried to kiss me again.

"What time is it?" Why was I asking that? "No, I just need to get home. Where am I?"

"We're in DC. You don't remember much of last night?"

"I remember it all," I lied, wishing that were true. "I was just confused about what neighborhood this is."

James, resigned to the fact that I was neither going to sleep with him or let him sleep, finally sat up. He got out of bed and was gone for a couple of minutes. I was desperate to get out of there. I checked my pocket. My ID and credit card were still there but I only had about $10 in cash. That wouldn't be enough to take a cab back to my apartment. And…I didn't have my keys! They were in the pocket of my jacket, which I'd left in Alec's car. I didn't even have the option of walking to my office.

"Can I use your phone to call my roommate to pick me up?" I asked when James got back.

"I can drive you in a while. Where do you live?"

"No, that's okay. I'm sure my roommate won't mind."

James brought me his phone and I called my apartment. It rang and rang. Eric must have spent the night at his girlfriend's place.

"No answer?" James asked.

No answer. No option. I was going to have to accept his offer to drive me home.

"No. Would you please drive me home?"

I wasn't sure how I would get into my apartment, but I'd contend with that later.

"Sure. Let's have breakfast first."

I was in deep distress: it felt like he was trying to delay my leaving with the hope that something might still happen. "I'm not hungry."

"Well, I am. I need some coffee and a little something to wake up."

I followed James to his kitchen, hoping I could hurry him along.

"Coffee?" he offered.

I shook my head "no". All I could think was, "What if tries to drug me?" Instead, I stood there nervously while James ate his frozen waffle and gulped down some coffee.

When he was finally ready to go, we walked outside to his car and I got into the passenger seat with apprehension. I gave James directions and, about 25 minutes later, we were almost at my apartment. "After we go through the light up ahead, it's the second left."

"I work just down the street. Let me show you where."

What was this all about?

"No, that's okay," but we had passed my street. Where he was taking me?

James turned to me as we stopped at the next light. "You know, you're really lucky I'm not a rapist or murderer."

"Lucky," I thought, "what the hell does that mean?" I should have gotten out of the car, but the light changed and the car turned. We went several blocks and James pointed to a building on the right.

"That's my office." He pulled into the parking lot. I was panicked about what he might be planning.

"Okay, I really want to go home now!"

"Sure. Why don't you give me your number so we can go out again?" He handed me a piece of paper and a pen.

I wrote down a fake number while we drove back down the street and told James I lived in a different building than I did. I jumped out of the car as soon as it stopped.

When he drove away, I walked to the community building for my apartment complex. Eric still wasn't home, so I'd have to wait for the office to open to pay to have the property manager let me into the apartment since I didn't have my keys.

I got into my apartment around 10 and called Alec. I dispensed with any pleasantries.

"My keys are in my jacket in your car."

Alec said, "I know."

We made arrangements for him to stop by so I could get them.

While I waited, my anger intensified. Alec left me incapacitated with someone I'd just met a bar, late at night, knowing that I might not be able to get into my apartment! I <u>was</u> lucky that, while I had been scared, nothing had happened to me. It was clear to me from the way that Alec had behaved the night before that he was acting out of jealousy and not friendship.

Alec didn't see it that way.

"You were drunk. What was I supposed to do?"

"Go with me! Or, at least, stay and talk me into going home." Honestly, Alec could have literally picked me up and carried me a block and that separation from James would have worked.

"That guy was a jerk."

There was that jealousy. "Yes, and I <u>was</u> drunk. I had no idea what I was doing."

"Well," Alec said, "maybe you shouldn't drink so much." He placed the evening on my shoulders.

Alec left and I cried. I was still angry that Alec had left me stranded with a stranger. But I was too embarrassed to talk to anybody about it. I shouldn't have had so much to drink.

I shouldn't have had so much to drink. I shouldn't have. I shouldn't have let someone buy me drinks at a bar. I shouldn't have gone somewhere with a stranger.

What about what Alec shouldn't have done? He shouldn't have tried to coopt me into being on a date. He shouldn't have left me in such a dangerous situation. I thought that I was lucky, that I could count on my friend.

I shouldn't have. Maybe, I shouldn't have gone somewhere alone with Alec.

An Image of Womanhood

Bushra Jabre

My first experience in Saudi Arabia was arriving at the airport in Jeddah in 1985. I looked around in the terminal building and became aware that I was the only single woman there. The few women that were in the terminal were all in black accompanied by men in white robes. I felt people looking at me. I charged ahead and went to the immigration desk.

I wore a long blue skirt and long sleeved jacket but did not cover my hair, which at that time was thick, curly, long, and black. I handed my passport to the Immigration Officer. He looked at the visa and looked at me.

"Where is your Mahram?"

I was not familiar with the term and asked him, "What do you mean?"

He looked at me with disgust and said, "Your husband."

I said, "I am not married."

He said, "Your father?"

I said, "My father died many years ago."

He said, "Your brother?"

I said, "I do not have any brothers."

He said, "Your uncle?"

I said, "Why would my uncle travel with me?"

The officer had an anguished look on his face; he waived me to stand aside. I did not understand what the problem was. I waited for about ten minutes and went back and asked him for my passport. He asked me why I was coming to Saudi Arabia. I thought that if I told him UNICEF, he would not know what that was, so I said that I was coming to work with the Presidency for Girls Education. He developed a disgusted look on his face. Once again, he waved me away. I went to the representative of the Saudi Arabia airline and told him what happened.

He said, "As you are travelling on to Riyadh, you will find your passport there."

"How do I know that it will be there?"

He looked at me in a strange way and walked away.

I had no other recourse than to proceed to the flight going to Riyadh, with my thoughts going in all directions.

"What if they kept my passport in Jeddah? What if I was arrested in Riyadh, as I did not have a passport? What if there was no one from UNICEF waiting for me at the airport?"

The flight time was about two hours of worry and anguish. I finally arrived in Riyadh to find Tom, the UNICEF representative waiting for me in the arrival zone.

"How was your flight?"

"The flight was good, but the arrival was puzzling," I said.

When I reported what happened with the immigration officer in Jeddah, he exploded with laughter. When I told him that I did not catch the joke, he told me that the visa I had was a special visa. It seems that the royal princes usually provide this type of visa to their girlfriends, so when the officer asked me why I was in Saudi Arabia and I told him to work with the Presidency of Girls Education, he thought that I was pulling his leg, as all the teachers working for the presidency had to observe a stringent dress code with full face cover. There I was with uncovered hair and regular dress telling him that I would be working with the most conservative structure in the country.

"He probably thought that you were making fun of him and that you had a powerful person backing you. That is why he did not know what to do."

"How do I get my passport?"

He said, "Let me go and get it."

He was away for about twenty minutes and came back with my passport in his hand. I was so relieved to get it back.

I took my passport and kept looking at it to make sure that it was still valid and no strange stamps were put on it.

Later on that evening, the wife of the UNICEF representative gave me an Abaya, and told me that I should wear it whenever I went out.

"You will get used to it," she informed me. "We all did."

Accommodation in Saudi Arabia

I thought that UNICEF would put me in a hotel. When Tom, the UNICEF representative informed me that no single woman could go to a hotel alone, I asked, "So where will I stay?"

"At your cousin's house."

My cousin was working in the same office as a technical advisor.

"That is very nice, but what if I did not have a cousin in Riyadh?"

"We would have had to figure that one out."

Staying with my cousin Ibrahim's family proved to be very convenient and pleasant. His wife, Sana, is a cheerful person, whereas he is the serious type. She was my shopping companion and my social director, inviting people that I knew from Lebanon and connecting me with her social network.

I discovered the difficulty of mobility for women in Saudi Arabia. I could not drive a car, take a taxi, or use public transport. To go to my meetings, the presidency provided me with a car and a driver. All the drivers were Moutaween (members of the religious police). The driver assigned to me was called Saad. He came to get me every morning and took me to the office and brought me back in the evening. At first, he would not look at me, address me or answer any questions. Slowly, I began to tell him what I was doing in Saudi Arabia and how important it was for the health of the mothers and children. Slowly I gained his trust and we began to have long discussions on children and ways of raising them.

One day I got into the car and Saad drove away. I discovered that I had left my Abaya at home.

I said, "Amm Saad, please go back, I forgot my Abaya."

He turned and looked at me and said, "As if you wear it properly."

I had to admit that the Abaya I was wearing was a bit short and, in most instances, I had it draped over my shoulders like a cap.

I did not cover my face and, in some instances, I forgot to cover my hair. Every time I went the compound of the Presidency of Girls Education, the guard at the gate mumbled something. I knew it was related to my uncovered face, so one time I just stood in front of him and said,

"With all due respect Amm, every time I pass by you, I hear you saying things that are not nice. If you do not like what you see, do not look at me. Thank you."

He was so surprised that he just looked at me with his mouth open. I walked away thinking it was probably the first time a woman dared to confront him. I did not fit his idea of the submissive woman. My colleagues at the

Presidency were horrified by what I did. As I was a visitor, I could do that and get away with it.

I was not so lucky in Qaseem, a province in Saudi Arabia that is the home of Wahhabism, the most conservative brand of Islam. I visited Qaseem among other governorates of the Kingdom armed with a letter from UNICEF saying that my travel was related to work with the Presidency of Girls Education.

I stepped off the plane and walked towards the terminal. I heard shrieking voices. I said to myself, there must have been a dead person on the plane and they are bringing the corpse to bury it in Breida, the capital. It did not occur to me that I was the one who instigated these noises. All of a sudden, I saw a black piece of cloth falling on me and I tripped over my long dress and nearly fell flat on my face.

The women who were waiting for me and who threw that material on me, told me that I should cover my face with it immediately. I said I couldn't see or breathe, as the material that was made of synthetic fiber. I was rushed into the car and driven to the guesthouse where I was to stay.

The guesthouse was in the same compound with a school for girls. It was a pleasant, comfortable villa. The Presidency provided me with transport, a GMC driven by one of the religious police and accompanied by his wife, who acted as a chaperone. As the driver cannot be alone with a woman in the car, his wife accompanies him and is paid by the Presidency for playing the chaperone's role. I had to learn how to get in and out of GMC car that is a high SUV wearing a long skirt and an Abaya, covering my hair with a long shawl and carrying my briefcase and my handbag. It was an art to be mastered. I was glad that I did not have to endure this all my life.

One afternoon, one of the school principals accompanied me to Breida's souk for shopping. We went into several stores and it was time for the sunset prayer. The shop salesman asked us to leave the shop immediately. All the store doors closed down. Fatima, my colleague said, "Let us go and wait in the nearby garden as the stores will open soon after the prayer was over." So we went to the near public garden and sat waiting for the prayer to end. It took about fifteen minutes and we saw one Mutawaa accompanied by two policemen passing by. They turned around and came back and stood in front of me. The cleric started saying something. I could not understand what he said. I remembered the advice of a friend, "If you are alone or with another woman and were apprehended by a Mutawaa, raise your voice, as he would be scared from people congregating around him. A woman can accuse him of harassing her."

"Are you a foreigner?" the Mutawaa asked.

I said, "No, I am an Arab and a Moslem."

He said, "Your stockings are not thick enough."

I looked at him and said, "You mean to tell me that during the Prophet's time, women used to wear stockings?? And how come you saw my stockings? My long dress is covering my legs!!"

He cursed me and walked on. I did not fit his image of how a woman should respond.

I looked for Fatima and could not find her. She had disappeared.

I walked around the public garden and saw Fatima looking in the direction where we were sitting. I asked her "How come you disappeared?"

She told me that women are afraid of these self-appointed religious police as they have a free hand in dealing with the citizens. She preferred to leave me alone to deal with him, as he would probably not dare treat me badly, being a foreign woman on her own, whereas he would mistreat a Saudi woman. Once again, I thanked God that I am not a Saudi woman.

The Presidency of Girls Education

The history of this governmental structure goes back to the 1970s when King Feisal wanted to push girls' education but met with the resistance of the traditional leaders. He compromised by assigning the education of girls that is encouraged in Islam, to the religious leaders. A structure parallel to the Ministry of Education was set up to cater to the education of girls. Parents were given stipends to encourage them to send their girls to schools and the police force in some locations used to escort the buses transporting the girls from their homes to the schools to protect them from the angry men who were opposed to their education.

The result was that the majority of girls in Saudi Arabia were enrolled in schools and today, women have a higher enrollment rate than men in colleges and universities despite the limited opportunities for women in the workforce. However, it became evident that women needed help for ensuring better health for themselves and their children.

My experience with the presidency came through UNICEF who asked me to develop a curriculum for mother and child health education through the school curricula and the adult literacy education program. I was the regional Advisor for Health Communication and Women's programs at the UNICEF Regional Middle East and North Africa Office. This assignment provided a challenge for me and I accepted to take it on. In developing this program, I worked with Saudi colleagues from the Presidency. I got to know the obstacles and constraints that limited women from accessing health services and taking care of their health. I designed the program based on the research findings. At the Presidency, the women directors, from Lebanon and Syria as well as the Saudis, had to defer to the male directors and they communicated by phone. They never met. It was not allowed. I never met with any of these male directors.

One of my technical assistance visits consisted of training Saudi women directors of school districts in conducting literacy education classes based on mother and child health themes. I had developed the manual but to put it in practice, I had to train the trainers who would later train the teachers on applying the lessons through interactive methods, which were new to all of them. The challenging task was to get the directors together in the capital Riyadh. It was the first time that such an event would be organized by the Presidency for its staff.

"How would they travel alone without their Mahram?" (Blood-related male) "Where would we put them?"

This took a lot of working out and finally, and for the first time, the women travelled alone and were accommodated in a hotel. There were forty participants and on every floor, they positioned a guard from the religious police

(Mutawaa) to make sure that no infractions were committed.

The participants were bused to the conference hall where the training was held in the morning and returned to the hotel in the afternoon.

They were happy to be away from home and office. Being in a group has its advantages in creating new friendships, but also close living created friction. One evening I got a phone call from one of the participants asking me to come over to sort out a conflict between two participants. As I was staying with my cousin, I asked him to drive me to the hotel, which was very close to where he lived. I asked him to drop me off at the hotel and that I would find my own way back.

I had to listen to the various versions of the misunderstanding and mediate the differences. It took a couple of hours to sort out the issue and reconcile the differences. All the women joined us in the lounge and started interrogating me.

"Where do you live?"

"In Paris."

"Where is your husband?"

"I am not married."

"So you live with your parents in Paris?"

"No, I live alone."

"You mean all by yourself?"

"Yes, all by myself."

The look on their faces was complete astonishment.

"Aren't you afraid of living alone?"

"No, I am not afraid."

"How do you live in Paris?"

I could see how they may have imagined me dancing the French can-can at the Moulin Rouge.

"I live like any other person, I have many friends. I travel to visit my family in Lebanon and to work in different countries."

"How does your family accept that?"

"My mother comes and visits me. I also visit her several times a year. We are quite close and she is more like a friend."

From the looks on their faces, I felt as though I might as well be from Mars. It was so unusual for them to see an

Arab woman who is independent and a professional working on international programs and travelling alone. I was such a novelty that they wanted to ask the most intimate things.

"Why are you not married?"

"How does your family accept that you stay unmarried?"

"How do people in your community accept you?"

It was around 11 p.m. when I finished. I did not want to call my cousin to come and get me. As his house was about a ten-minute walk from the hotel, I thought I would walk back. The women asked me if my car was waiting for me and I told them I was going to walk home. They looked at me as if I was crazy and one woman said, "You cannot do that."

"Why not?"

"No woman walks alone, especially not at night."

I said, "Watch me."

I went down to the reception and the hotel staff, helpful as always, asked me "Madam, where is your driver?"

I said, "I do not have one and I am walking."

"What? No, no you cannot do that!"

"Yes, I can."

I walked out of the hotel and looked back. On the third floor, all the windows had black figures looking out. On the first floor, all the hotel staff were looking out and gesturing for me to go back to the hotel. It was a very funny scene.

I walked and it was no longer funny. Every single car that passed by stopped to pick me up. The drivers were insistent and followed me offering to take me for a ride. I pretended not to understand what was being said and kept walking annoyed and afraid. I kept thinking, "What if one grabs me and pulls me into the car? How can I defend myself? I could hit him with my briefcase. Would anyone come to rescue me?" My heart was pounding and I walked quickly praying to God to help me arrive safely. It was the first and last time I walked alone down a street in Saudi Arabia. Once again, I was glad that I was only visiting the Kingdom and did not have to put up with this all my life.

A few months after the training, I was asked by the Presidency to follow-up on the local trainings. This provided me with a unique experience of visiting the various regions of the Kingdom. I travelled with a letter from UNICEF explaining that I was an international staff member working with the Presidency of Girls Education. My assignment was to assess educational programs in the provinces. I had to show the letter at airports and whenever I was asked what I was doing.

There are advantages for a woman travelling alone in Saudi Arabia. She is given priority in airports and in airplane seating. She does not have to queue and is given preferential service. However, it is problematic for a single woman to stay in a hotel on her own. In those days, to do so required a letter from the police. My guess was that it certified that the woman was not a prostitute. In all the provinces, I was hosted in guesthouses run by the Presidency. Luckily this regulation is no longer in force since 2000.

Al Qaseem

Al Qaseem is the home province of Mohammad Ben Abdel Wahab, the Patron of Wahhabism, the most conservative form of Islam and the official sect of Saudi Arabia. I was told that home lease contracts stipulate that the head of the household should attend daily prayer at the community mosque and that in Mosques they would take roll calls to make sure everyone in the neighborhood was present at all prayers. I was also told that they used to raise a flag on the house if there is a young woman in the household ready to be married off. I had no way of verifying this.

Hussa, the Director of Girls Education in Al Qaseem, told me about her experience as one of the first group of girls to attend school in her province. Her father was a prominent judge and people ridiculed him for sending his daughter to school. Men would throw stones at the bus carrying the girls to school and at the girls directly when they arrived at school. Police escorted the bus to ensure the girls' safety.

Hussa said, "It was tough, but we did it and here I am now directing a high school. It was not easy, but we opened the door to all Saudi women and now they are in business and academia."

Mecca

The driver that assigned to take me around in Mecca was an unfriendly person. He was sullen and kept complaining that we are taking a lot of time in our meetings and professional visits. Amani, my Syrian/Saudi counterpart, was a funny woman. She joked a lot while riding to our meetings. The driver, Amm Mohammad warmed to us and started slowly participating in the discussions.

On Friday, he picked me up and we drove to Jeddah airport. The drive was about one hour, and throughout the drive Amm Mohammad asked me questions about what his wife should do: contraception, raising children, nutrition. I was so gratified that he felt comfortable enough to ask me these questions which meant that he understood what I was doing in Saudi Arabia and was interested enough to see how it applied to his family welfare.

When he dropped me off at the airport, he wished me a safe journey and told me that his wife was pregnant and if he gets a daughter, he will call her after me. I called my colleagues and told them this and they were so surprised and said miracles can happen.

Saudi Update

In December 2011, I received an invitation from the Ministry of Health to participate in a conference in Riyadh organized by the Ministry of Health and Sohatna, a nongovernmental organization for health promotion. I thought they must be confused and thought that I was a male. The name Bushra is given to males in Egypt and Sudan and I used to receive mail in the name of Mr. Bushra Jabre. I wrote them back saying that I am a female and are they sure they want to invite me, since it was difficult to secure visas for single women traveling to the Kingdom.

They responded by saying that they knew who I was and that I would be a guest of the government. They would arrange for my visa, travel and accommodation.

The topic of the conference intrigued me: Community Empowerment for Health Promotion. Since my understanding of empowerment clashes with the image that I had of the system in Saudi Arabia, I wrote them seeking clarification of what they meant by the term empowerment. I received a vague definition and decided to suggest that I give the main presentation of the conference on Community Empowerment.

I wrote a synopsis of the presentation and sent it for their review. They appreciated it and agreed that I give it as the keynote presentation. I suggested that I could also make a presentation on Women's Empowerment for Family Health, based on my work in Egypt, and a presentation on the Role of Religious Leaders as agents of change in family health, based on my work in Jordan.

The conference was held at the King Khalid Specialty Hospital. It has a vast campus with separate conference facilities and accommodations for the expatriate staff. I was accommodated in the guesthouse of the hospital where the conference was held. The morning of the conference, a young veiled woman came knocking on my door and accompanied me to the conference pavilion. I was impressed with the organization and the attention to detail.

I was pleasantly surprised in the conference that despite gender segregation norms in Saudi Arabia women and men attended the various sessions and participated on equal basis. Most of the women, physicians and health workers, were veiled with faces covered. That did not deter them from voicing their opinions and making presentations on their projects. I was quite astonished by the quality of the participation and the passion of the women in proving themselves. Two female physicians chaired two conference sessions very ably. Several young female physicians, but not males, approached me seeking information on how they could apply for PhD programs at Johns Hopkins University in Baltimore. The government of Saudi Arabia pays the tuition, accommodations, car and monthly stipends for its citizens who are accepted in any university in the United States or any other country.

Revisiting Abha, 25 years later

While attending the conference in Riyadh, I received a phone call from the World Health Organization representative in Saudi Arabia. I talked to him and he asked to meet me. We agreed that he would come to the hospital where I was staying before I left for the airport. In Saudi Arabia, there is no place for a woman and a man to meet, even in a Mall or a coffee shop, as there is the risk of the Mutawaa descending on the place and asking for IDs. If the couple was not married or related, prison is a possibility and the hassle would be a nightmare.

I walked to the hospital gate at the agreed time wondering how would I recognize him, when I saw a man in Moroccan robes waving to me from far. He turned out to be a director of health services at the Moroccan Ministry of Health that I had worked with twenty years ago in Rabat, Morocco.

Dr. Mostafa wanted me to participate in a national conference on Healthy Cities taking place in Abha, Aseer province the following week.

I was to leave on Friday evening to Riyadh, wait five hours at the airport to get another flight to Abha, arrive there at 6 a.m., give my presentation at 10 a.m., have a meeting that afternoon and catch a flight at 2 a.m. to arrive in Amman at midday.

I flew to Riyadh and was surprised that at the airport there was no separation of sexes in the lounges, and people were not surprised to see me travelling alone. Gone were the days when I used to have a letter explaining why I was travelling on my own without a Mahram.

I was met at the airport in Abha and taken to the hotel where the conference was held. Abha is a thriving city these days. I knew the place when it was a small town with a few streets. Now it has highways and many hotels and furnished apartments, as it is tourist destination of Saudi vacationers.

Arriving at the conference hall, I was told that I should enter through the female section. I said, "But I am going on the podium to make a presentation." I still was ushered to the women's section. In the large conference hall, a section was set aside for women participants by a screen cutting the conference room into two sections. It was obvious that the relaxation of the segregation code did not arrive in Aseer yet. I sat with the women until the time of my presentation when I went on to the podium and sat with the session speakers. I was wearing a long black coat and a scarf, which kept slipping off my head.

I made the presentation on Women Advocates for Mother and Child Health, the case of Egypt and Azerbaijan. The presentation solicited a great number of questions on the adaptability of the methodology to the Saudi context and within the Healthy Cities Initiative.

Lunchtime came and I went to the hotel restaurant. I sat with the male colleagues without thinking and found out that once again there was a separate section for women. Obviously, I was not respecting the local code of conduct, but nobody mentioned anything, and I got away with it.

In the afternoon, a visit was organized for the participants. Again, there was a bus for women and another for men. We were taken to Sauda, the highest peak in Aseer, which is more than 3,700 meters above sea level. There we boarded cable cars to take us down to the valley. The drop was spectacular but the shrieks of the women, who came from other provinces that are flat, were more dramatic. One was bemoaning her infant daughter whom she may not see again, another wondered if the tigers would eat us should we fall. I had to reassure her that there were no tigers in Saudi Arabia.

I returned to the hotel for my meeting with the people from the Ministry of Health and WHO. Once again, I defied the local code once again and sat with the male colleagues in the lobby café and had tea. What surprised me most was my acceptance by the Saudi male colleagues. They asked me direct questions and looked straight at me, something I would have never imagined twenty years ago. They requested my technical assistance in program planning and evaluation and in capacity building.

I had several hours to catch my flight to Amman, so I sat in the common lounge ignoring the sign that indicated the way to the women's lounge. I adopted a look that dared anyone who might approach me and ask me to move to the women's lounge. No one did. This was a long way from the time I used to transit in Jeddah on my way to Yemen. At that time, I was always afraid that they would put me in the women's lounge and lock the door and the flight would take off and I would be left behind. I was terrified with the thought of being stuck in such a patriarchal society where I would have no rights. I used to approach any man on the Middle East Airline flight from Beirut and ask to sit with him during the layover time. The men were always understanding and accommodating. This time I did not have to approach anyone. I just sat in the coffee shop and worked on my laptop. I was the only single woman around, but did not encounter any hassle.

Upon boarding the flight, a man approached me and asked me if I was a journalist. I asked him what made him think so. He said, "You were writing all the time." I said. "I am writing a book." He looked at me with astonishment. I just did not fit in his image of women.

My Ride on the Pussy Train

Mary Lucas

It happened in Mexico City in the winter of 1974. My classmates and I were traveling across Mexico ostensibly to study Mexican history and culture over our winter break from Lincoln Trail Junior College in my home town of Robinson, Illinois. At nineteen, it was my first trip to Mexico; the first time I ever escaped winter to play in the sun; and, on that fateful morning, the first time I rode a subway. It was worlds away from Robinson, a rural town of 7,200 people near the central Indiana border.

The population in Mexico City was just under 7 million at that time. It was a vibrant era in the city's history. People were well dressed and sophisticated and the place filled with the energy and sense of purpose that reminded me of the way London, Paris and New York looked in the movies. The juxtaposition of old and new was fascinating. A cathedral from the 1600s sat in Plaza Zocala, once a major Aztec gathering place now at the heart of a major modern city. We were enthralled with the city and excited about exploring in wider arcs from our hotel in the Zona Rosa. There were about a dozen of us and we had some scheduled class events with our instructor, but he was staying with his cousin in a neighborhood near our hotel, leaving us a generous amount of time on our own.

People in the city kept telling us we had to try their new subway system, opened in 1969. There was a station within easy walking distance from our hotel so we set out one morning to take the train for one stop. The new station was modern and gleaming. Our group was among the first passengers who lined up on the platform, oblivious to the growing crowds behind us. A train pulled up, let off its passengers, and we headed into a nearly empty car.

We spread out in the middle of the train car with some distance between us; many of us chose to stand. As it started to fill up the distance between my classmates grew as an endless stream of new passengers kept pushing into the car. Politely shuffling my feet initially to help the people around me settle into a spot gave way to being squashed against bodies pushing into me from all sides. I was hanging by one hand from a strap on the ceiling. Bodies kept pressing their way in until it felt as if each inch of space was filled. The doors closed.

At a height of 5'6", I was taller than most of the people around me. This ride was another first; my first experience being trapped in a crowd so tight I could literally not move. My left arm reached up to cling to the strap, while my right arm was trapped by my side protecting my purse.

Hanging there, I understood the phrase packed in like a sardine. We were only traveling to the next station but I had no idea how far the ride was or how long it would it take. We started a slow roll out of the station. I stared across the sea of heads and held on, already anxious for the ride to end.

As the train gained speed, a hand suddenly and violently grabbed my crotch. Clearly, the act was not an accident due to excessive crowding. It was a forceful, menacing, I mean business kind of grab. Startled, I looked down at a man with a huge paunch and a sweating, sneering face. He wore shapeless jeans, a cheap cotton shirt and a bad haircut, which all conspired to accentuate his unappealing visage. My eyes locked on his and I hissed in a near whisper, “Let go!”

My anger fueled his pleasure. I doubt he spoke English but I’m sure he understood the message. My attacker was a perverse opportunist who spotted a young woman in a mini skirt trapped in the middle of the car. He positioned his short self in front of me and waited until the train started to move. As the space kept filling up, I naively made as much room as possible around me so more people could fit into the packed space. I failed to pay attention to the people crowding in around me.

Anger and disgust were driving me and I hissed louder, “Get your hand off me.” I was half hoping someone would catch on to the situation; yet I was too stunned and embarrassed to start screaming or ask for help.

Again, I saw that my pleas were only adding to the thrill for him. He fed on my disgust as a parasite feeds on its host, draining my energy and marring my naïve view of a big, safe, happy world.

The thought flashed through my mind that this male (I will not call him a man) was likely ignored or scorned by most women. His body had the bulging lines of a heavy, middle-aged man, yet I doubt he was past thirty.

As the train hit full speed the car began to rock slightly and the beast's hand became more aggressive, kneading and bullying my pussy. Beads of sweat appeared along his prematurely receding hairline. I couldn't decide if it was caused by so many people being jammed together, or in response to his hand in my crotch. His eyes remained locked on mine as his fingers continued to grope. His gaze was defiant and downright mocking.

I felt nauseated and a little light headed; my blood pressure was likely soaring. The man's sadistic joy at my plight made me wonder how many women he had grabbed, and if he had inflicted much worse pain on other victims. He was evil.

It was unlikely I could escape before the train stopped. I knew no Spanish words to alert the passengers around me to my situation (and none of my classmates were close enough to help). I was so wedged into my position I could not move enough to get away from his probing hand. Plus, as much as I wanted to make him stop, I was embarrassed. I did not want people to watch the man violate me in this absurd way. My embarrassment only added to my anger, which only stepped up his pleasure.

As the ride went on, my disgust turned towards hate. I wanted revenge. I wanted him demeaned and embarrassed. My only hope of a satisfactory ending was to destroy the man's happy memory of our meeting. I had to hurt him. But how? Although the Mexico City subway was my first subway ride, I had ridden enough passenger trains to know that they jerk when the brakes take hold. I realized I only had to twist slightly to be in position to push into the man as we came to a stop.

As the train started to slow, I slightly rotated my right arm toward the front of my body, positioning it in front of my right side. My plan was to aim my bony elbow so I could push it down into the man's chest as the train jerked to a stop. Sadly, he was too short for me to reach his groin.

My squirming elated the man. He was visibly excited and the increased pressure of his hand combined with his growing smugness fed my determination to fight back.

When our train jerked forward as it stopped, I was able to move. I pulled myself up with the hand that was clinging to the roof bar and put the full force of my 98 pounds behind that spikey, bony little elbow, pushing it somehow down into the man's chest. Much to my amazement, I made a direct hit with more force that I thought possible. The doors of the subway opened and people began pouring out; but my eyes remained locked on the pervert's eyes as he dropped to his knees; his offensive, crotch grabbing hand joining his other hand to clutch his chest. I gave him a big gotcha look before he dropped his head and clutched his chest tighter. A few passengers stopped to help him; it looked like he was having a heart attack.

I wish I could see a video of that moment to understand how I brought him down. It happened so fast I don't know exactly how it worked. I will never know. Watching that rodent drop to his knees did not erase what he did to me; but it made me feel infinitely better. As my classmates started coming together in the crowd someone asked, "What's wrong with that man?"

"He grabbed my crotch and he wouldn't let go," I answered. "So, I elbowed him in the chest when the train stopped. Pervert." My tone was light and dismissive; but that is not how I felt about the attack.

Our group came back together as we headed for the exit. Throughout the day, various classmates asked about the man on the train, but I didn't want to talk about it. I wanted to leave it behind.

After it happened, I didn't have nightmares about him; I didn't have new fears of being in crowds; my life wasn't changed – with the exception of learning to pay more attention to what's going on around me. Yet I found myself carrying the memory around like extra baggage. Flashes of the experience would pop up at random moments and I relived the disgust and shame I felt because of what he did to me; I was angry at myself for getting into that situation. So, I worked at making it go away. Eventually, over time, it worked because I forgave myself. I was a victim; I could not escape. It was not my fault.

Dredging up the memories again after so many years, my recollections boiled down to the man, his hand, the crowd pressed around me, and the helplessness of being trapped. Most of all I remember my shock that any man would grab my pussy and take such pleasure in my revulsion. It was a vile act.

Today I understand the importance of fighting back for all women who are at risk of being manhandled and abused. That is my final retaliation. I'm sharing my story with no hesitation or embarrassment now because I understand that abuse will only be stopped when it no longer has a place to hide.

Christmas in Phoenix

Cheryl Shaver Kanuck

Part I

Now that I'm a "southerner," I am getting used to green Christmases, but in 1997 I experienced my first non-northern Christmas. I was in Phoenix, Arizona. It was as beige as it had been on all of my previous trips, with touches of cactus green, and the temperatures were in the '70s. I was there to spend Christmas with my daughter Samantha. That is, I hoped to spend Christmas with her, but I would not be certain of that until Christmas Eve. With or without snow, it would be a different kind of Christmas.

I anticipated a visit of one week, and had arranged to stay at a hotel with kitchenettes in the rooms that would be perfect for us. It was not far from the airport, and I thought it would be very convenient. As I drove to my lodgings, a sinking feeling seeped into my core. The neighborhood got seedier the closer I got and, when I saw the hotel itself, my heart plummeted. It was covered with layers of chipping, with over-bright paint trying to hide the tracks of time. This was not the place to start a new life. I had to find a way out of this.

I stopped at the office and asked if there was a map of the city I could look at so I might determine the relative position of this place in the greater Phoenix area. Of course, in accordance with my hastily devised 'escape' plan, the map showed me that this location was not going to be convenient for me after all. In a very hospitable manner, the woman behind the desk gave me the name of another extended-stay facility, and even gave me the map, with the route to the other location clearly marked in orange highlighter.

I drove there with a quivery feeling I could only compare to stage fright, praying silently that this was not going to be another disaster. I pulled up in front of the second hotel. It was lovely, and in a much nicer neighborhood, on a thoroughfare that would give me ready access to anywhere I might need to go. The trembling in my gut subsided as the tour of the grounds revealed a beautiful courtyard, with trees and vibrantly blooming shrubs, in the center of a square of two-story stucco buildings. Breakfast was available at a small café in the complex for only one additional dollar per person per day. I had found our "home" for the next week. As soon as I unpacked, I called the prison.

Two rings. A husky voice. "Arizona Women's Prison. Can I help you?"

"Hello, I'm calling with regard to my daughter, Samantha Jones. I'm in Phoenix and hoping to pick her up for Christmas. You should have a notarized letter from me in her file. Thank you – yes, I can hold."

After an eternity, the voice returned and told me her release was on the schedule. I can pick her up at 5 a.m. on Christmas morning. I was so grateful I could barely speak, but somehow I croaked out my next few questions: "Is there anything I need to do? Shall I come into the building to pick her up? Do I need to sign anything? Yes, I have a local contact number." I gave them the number from the phone in my room. "Thank you. This will be a very special Christmas. Goodbye." The tears in my eyes spilled the moment I hung up.

Now I only had one day to wait, I told myself, but I would keep busy preparing for Christmas. First, I found the supermarket and bought everything I needed for a nice Christmas dinner, and for a week of possible lunches, dinners or evening snacks. At the drug store in the same plaza, I found a small artificial Christmas tree and lights. I decided against the expense of other tree decorations – strings of miniature white lights would be perfect. I returned to the room to put away the food, and left the tree and lights there, so I could go back out to purchase presents.

This Christmas required practical gifts, first because my daughter had nothing – literally nothing – and second because I had no money for anything that was not truly needed. Drugs had stolen everything from her, and nearly taken her life. If I went to every pawn shop in Phoenix, would I find traces of the past? My grandmother's amethyst pendant? The birthstone ring that was Samantha's 18th birthday present from me? The gold and diamond butterfly pendant that my brother gave me on my 21st birthday – passed on to her because he was her godfather? It broke my heart to think of these. But these are nothing compared to her life. At least she still had that.

What did you need to start a life from scratch? Clothing, linens, an iron, a hair dryer, brush and comb – no she should pick some of these out herself. Questioning my choices at every turn, I eventually amassed the bare beginnings of a life – at least those things that might reasonably be considered presents. And I bought wrapping paper, ribbon, tape and scissors – she could keep the tape and scissors too.

Wrapping the gifts was a bittersweet task. This was so unlike past Christmases when gifts were meant to surprise and delight. I felt so sad. I placed the gifts under the tree, then went out to get my luggage to unpack the little gifts

I brought with me from home – gifts I had purchased for her over the last few years when I did not know where she was or whether she was still alive: a delicate chain with a pendant signifying long life, a blank journal with a pretty pen, a silk scarf, her favorite perfume – was it still her favorite, I wondered. Small items – one for each missed Christmas and birthday, five years' worth. These, too, went under the tree. She would know I never stopped loving her. Then I went to bed, but sleep did not come easily.

To pick her up at 5:00 a.m., I needed to be up at 3:30. A quick shower – no breakfast. I studied the map and memorized the route. Arriving early, I purchased two French Vanilla cappuccinos for us, and a single red rose for her at the Circle K convenience store across from the Arizona State Women's Prison. It was dark and chilly. I drove through the gate into the prison parking area and waited. At 5:05, a group of about 20 women began to walk out of the building and disperse into the arms of waiting loved ones. In five more minutes, Samantha was standing next to my car smiling. I put her single cardboard box of possessions on the back seat, and we embraced. We drove home making small talk. I didn't cry.

When we entered our room, the little Christmas tree was sparkling with a hundred tiny white lights, just as I had left it. I held her and whispered "Merry Christmas."

"Merry Christmas, Mom. Thank you for coming."

"Where else would I be, sweetheart? I love you."

"I know – but thanks."

Part II

Christmas day was over and we lay in the double bed, ready for sleep. It had gone well, though not without its awkward moments, each of us sometimes unsure how to act or what to say. It was a strange way to feel with my own child. The obligatory phone calls to loved ones seemed to go smoothly, and the dinner was comforting in its familiarity. But there was a hollow, anxious feeling I couldn't shake. Sleep would make it better.

In the dark, she spoke. "Mom – I know this is a lot to ask, but have you decided about what we talked about on the phone last week?"

"Yes." I paused. "I think that if this is something important to you – if you're sure you're up to it yourself – then we should go."

"But what about you?"

"I don't expect it to be easy, but I'll be fine. Remember Sweetie, you chose this couple and gave them a magnificent gift. And remember too that they chose an open adoption. Call Tina in the morning; ask what is a good time for them, and we'll make a day of it." I lightly squeezed her hand. I prayed that I really could be fine with this. Would I be able to see and hold this baby, my first-born grandchild, without falling to pieces?

Part III

The day appointed for our visit to Tucson, Saturday December 27, was sunny and mild. We dressed for a good first impression, my daughter more than me. She looked lovely in a skirt, modest blouse and warm white corduroy blazer. I wore an unassuming sweater and skirt in pink, wanting to appear completely nonthreatening. It wasn't about me anyway. I just needed to be reassuring to everyone, including myself.

We decided to make a recreational stop before our official business, thinking it would be good for both our nerves. We went nine miles southwest of Tucson to the San Xavier Mission. The 200-year-old church, set in the desert on an Indian reservation, was a bright white presence in the vast expanse of sand and sage. I hoped to find a morsel of peace there to appease my uneasy spirit, and hers.

The Mission was beautiful – serene – inside and out. The grounds were peaceful. In contrast, the parking lot was ringed by Native American food stands, peopled by the natives and their noisy playful children, and we treated our bodies to the warm satisfaction of eating their hot cinnamon-drenched fry-bread. Perhaps the bread fortified us, as much as the sacred surroundings.

As the time for our appointment neared, we left San Xavier and drove to a suburb outside of Tucson, following the detailed directions my daughter received on the telephone. The area felt as familiar as any suburb in the northeast, with shopping malls, tree-lined streets, small starter houses, and large executive homes. We found their street, and parked under a tree in front of their one-story home.

"Are you ready?"

"I think so."

"Shall we ring the bell?"

"Let's go."

The last few yards felt like a mile to me as we walked to the door. I rang the bell, and a young man answered. Tall, blonde Brian, a Johnson from Minnesota; he smiled and invited us in. He introduced himself, his wife Tina, and Tina's mother who was visiting for the holiday. I introduced myself and Samantha. It was shocking to me how much Tina resembled my daughter, and I commented that the two of them could almost be sisters.

Everyone smiled, except the mother – a grandmother to the child Samantha and I came to see. She was wary, and I didn't blame her – I thought I would be wary too, in her situation. I wished I looked more fashionable at that moment, feeling a bit dowdy in comparison. But I reminded myself this was not about me.

After a few minutes of small talk – the kind one uses when meeting a new neighbor – the moment arrived.

"It's about time for the baby to wake up for her next feeding. I thought you might like to feed her – that's why I suggested this time to you," Tina said sweetly.

"Would you like to feed her, Sweetie?" I asked my daughter.

"You first, Mom."

Tina left the room and returned in a minute with a tiny bundle, wrapped in a soft pink flannel blanket. The infant had delicate black curls encircling her elfin face. Her skin was translucent, latte-colored. "This is Sarah," Tina said, and handed her to me.

I held the baby in the crook of my left arm so her face was toward my daughter, letting her absorb the sight of her own child – the child she surrendered to these people at birth, just two weeks ago. My first grandchild. The daughter of my daughter. Which one pulled hardest on my heart at that moment? Which one called to my soul? Not this child who was the answer to a prayer for the Johnsons. Yes, I loved her unconditionally, but the child of my own body still needed a mother – still needed me. She needed me to be strong and to survive until the bottom fell out again. My daughter needed me to be standing when the dust settled. Sarah had a family to love her. Sarah was safe.

The visit ended. We drove back to Phoenix, and I spent the next few days trying to create a new life for my child. I was trying mightily not to leave her with only the streets to return to. Clothing, a job, an apartment. It all fell into place. On our last day together, a good friend came to the hotel to pick her up and help her move into the little apartment. We hugged, said "I love you," and then she was gone. I drove to the airport with tears in my eyes and dread in my heart. I lived a thousand miles away. It was the hardest Christmas of my life, at least up until then.

But the story was not over.

In three months, the bottom fell out. My daughter was gone. Again.

My Father Wore a Grey Suit

Dawn M. Gross, MD, PhD

My father wore a grey business suit. Sometimes, it was a three-piece, with an elegant tie and matching pocket scarf. He wore it every day. My mother always wore a two-piece suit with a skirt and matching lapel pin. She still does, except for Fridays. First, that was because it was "casual day." Now in her mid-seventies, it is because she prefers pants, plus, that is the day she works from home.

My father fully supported my mother's wearing of business suits at a time few women were welcome in the corporate world. In truth, mother's success was so profound that she ultimately supported my father's wearing of business suits throughout his career. They were a true team – even taking turns earning their respective MBAs. And while this kind of career equality was unusual in the late 1960s, it was our one and only reality.

My brother and I were raised in a dual-working parent household. We were latchkey and TV dinner kids. We knew no different.

When it came to soothing skinned knees or my brush with appendicitis, my parents' roles remained dual. My father hugged and my mother investigated. My father was an emotional reservoir and my mother, to this day, remains a woman of action.

Both encouraged me to follow my dreams. To live the mantra my maternal grandfather instilled in me: When you love what you do, you will never work a day in your life.

I grew up dreaming I would walk in my mother's footsteps. I pined over her suits. Her closet looked like a rainbow of elegance, each suit hung, color-coded with its uniquely designated lapel-pin. I tried to imagine what I would be doing, what I must have accomplished by the time I would get to wear such suits every day.

She took me to the Pacific Stock Exchange one morning. I hadn't yet reached puberty. It was loud with small pieces of paper scattered all over the floor. I had no idea what was happening. Men were yelling. I saw no other women. Still, for a short period of time, when someone would ask me what I wanted to be when I grew up, my answer was a trader.

My mother never spoke of glass-ceilings. The only obstacle my mother would ever invoke in my aspiration for medical school admittance would be numerical.

"Statistically speaking," she told me, "the odds are simply not in your favor." I never viewed myself as any different from a male applicant at that point in time. Yet even before I was admitted, the discrimination began.

During one of my medical school interviews, I was asked if I had any thoughts on abortion. My response, "Yes, I have thoughts." This was an illegal question that I later verified none of my co-interviewees that day, all of who were men, were asked.

When I met my future husband the second day of medical school, I was euphoric, and concerned. I had previously decided I needed to be financially independent before I could be ready for marriage. I wasn't looking for love. I had a minimum of another eight years of school ahead of me. When it became clear Andy was the one, I reached out to my father to ask what to do with this unexpected relationship. His soulful reply, "When you have a protracted educational path, you need to reconsider your definition of what it means to be an adult." In other words, he taught me that life is now and never meant to be put on hold. Fortunately, Andy was of the same mindset when I proposed.

When my husband and I chose to start our family during medical school my parents were fully supportive. Yet, I had no maternal instinct. I barely realized I was pregnant with my first child. In fact, it was my husband who alerted me, and our parents, that I was in labor. When our daughter was born, it was not love at first sight. It was shock. Even terror. I had been training my whole life to become a professional. I had been training the last eight years to become a physician-scientist. I had absolutely no training to become a parent.

It was simply a given that I would not mention my new role as "mother" during my medical residency interviews. Instead, I donned my carefully selected interview suit, with matching lapel pin, and carried as stealth a briefcase that I could find to hold the smallest portable breast pump available on the market. While colleagues made small talk between interviews, I excused myself to a toilet stall so I could relieve my milk ducts before they exposed my secret.

Had a residency program director learned of my eight-week-old daughter, I would have been dubbed, "uncommitted."

Four weeks later, something I was wholly unprepared for, happened. While rocking my daughter to sleep, I began to weep. My entire body shook and it felt as if every cell were screaming out, "I did not become a mother to let another person raise my child."

I had completed my residency interviews and my unofficial maternity leave. It was the night before I was to resume my clinical rotations of my last year of medical school. In the morning, I was to bring Isabell to daycare for the first time.

Don't get me wrong; our daycare was wonderful. We had no idea how fortunate we were. The facility had an exceptional reputation, it had availability exactly when we needed it, and it was located inside the hospital where my husband and I trained.

Isabell and I both survived our first day apart. We survived two months of rotations and daycare with little difficulty. I learned to pump in bathrooms, parked cars, and even while nursing. We seemed to have found a groove

Yet the day when my rank-list was due, the list that would be matched against the residency program interviews from a few months earlier, the list that would commit me to becoming an intern wherever the computer computed, I hesitated.

I was in distress, more distress than the night before my return to rotations and Isabell's entry into daycare. It was the only time I ever called an anonymous student-crises help line.

A woman whom I will never know answered the phone. I explained why I was calling, that I did not know what to do, and that I did not want to disappoint my mother and my PhD advisor, (a very accomplished scientist who happened to be a mother of three). "They believed in me," my hand shook as tears began to cover the phone handset. "They spent so much time and energy on me. If I stop and become a mother, it just feels like, they'll think I'm throwing it all away. That I am letting everyone down."

Her response was calm and without expectation or judgment. "If you were the only person on the planet. No one could see you. No one could say anything about what you do. What do you see yourself doing?"

Without hesitation I responded, "I see myself walking down the sidewalk on a sunny day with my daughter in a stroller."

"I think you've made your decision."

I hung up the phone and went straight to the program director of the hospital where my daughter was in daycare, where my husband was a resident and where I had done many of my medical school clinical rotations. I was a known entity with nothing to hide. "Would you want me if I applied next year?" A smile was all I needed.

I withdrew from the match.

I completed my clinical rotations and graduated two months later holding my daughter in my arms as I walked across the stage to receive my doctorates.

Shortly thereafter, I gave birth to my second child, and wouldn't have been surprised if I felt my life was complete. Instead, I was feeling something more than incompetent, exhausted and overwhelmed. Those feelings were all too familiar as a medical and graduate student. What I was feeling was un-whole.

As the months passed and July approached, I could not wait to start my residency. During the nights on-call, I was the happiest intern in my class, because I knew I was far more likely to get more sleep when I was in the hospital as compared to when I was at home.

Choosing to continue my training back inside a hospital that already knew me as a multi-dimensional person, married and maternal, physician and scientist, was remarkable. The hierarchy of medicine was quickly leveled each time my kids shared birthday parties with one of my supervising physicians. My bosses were no more expert about parenting than I. Children are the immediate equalizer.

So it was not until I was in a different hospital, as my career advanced, where I worked with people who did not already know me as all these things, or worse, didn't care, that being a mother became an obstacle.

Medicine has unique challenges. The obvious is when a patient is in extreme distress. It is hard to imagine any provider leaving for another commitment in the midst of a medical emergency. The more hidden challenges are related to the hierarchy of medical training: medical students, interns, residents and fellows are all trainees and have little, though increasing, autonomy as it relates to the actual practice of medicine. Having children does not change either of these realities.

My mother demonstrated that being a professional in no way negated one's ability to be a parent. Whenever I called her office as a child, no matter what meeting she was in, she took my call. Which is why my increasing isolation as a mother climbing my own career ladder came as such a shock.

Entering into an evening meeting, the dozen, classic high-backed leather chairs surrounding a long, dark wood table, were each occupied by men. I forced myself to lean in and take a seat. Eventually two other women joined me at the table. I subsequently learned that the other two did not have children. Part way through the meeting, one man publicly excused himself so he could attend his child's event. Everyone cooed him with support. At the end of the meeting, without a word, each of the men left and I and the other two women stayed behind to clean up the food. This happened every meeting.

And while I recognize this does not happen everywhere, certain stereotypes seem harder to break. My husband, a very devoted and fully engaged partner and parent, has rarely been called first when one of our children is sick. Even when his name is listed as first contact specifically while I am traveling several hundred miles from home, I still get the calls to come pick up our child.

Despite these persistent challenges, I was achieving all I set out to, all I could imagine. No glass ceiling was thwarting my ascent.

But here's the thing about a glass ceiling: you cannot see it as you approach.

Upon impact, I quickly discovered I am not made of steel. The chards cut me to the core as my very identity was brought into question. Am I a professional <u>or</u> a mother?

My husband has never been asked this question. Nor will he. I suspect my colleagues around the table were never asked this question. Nor will they. My father would have coveted the opportunity to respond.

My mother responded by sharing that she had, in fact, lost her first job in finance when she became pregnant. And, while the lawsuit she raised ultimately offered vindication, she never regained that job. She was simply told never to return.

Fifty years later, some things have yet to change. So in order to thrive, I have learned to seek out rare environments that embrace my whole self.

Many of my most joyful moments as a physician have included the intentional presence of one or more of my children. My two older ones have become hospice volunteers and visited with several of my patients while I tended to the care of others. And my youngest was able to join me on nearly all my home visits for the first year of his life. I often said he was the most powerful medicine I had and patients, families and staff concurred.

I also have to acknowledge the role friends, family and, most importantly, my husband have played in creating a team success. Of course, children teach you to become efficient in practice and flexible in thinking. And friends and family have been invaluable when we have needed extra hands to help care for our children until our work in the hospital was complete. And the gift of a double stroller with seat belts cannot be overstated when needing to bring young children to work.

These experiences are what help me live my grandfather's mantra today. They allow me to bring my whole self, not just my medical training, to the care of a whole person, not just their illness. And the team of my mother and father and their approach to parenting remains my role model.

My mother's suits are a rainbow of elegance. My father's suits were always a soft grey. His empathy was softer still. So this is the suit I seek to wear, to model what is possible and to graciously observe what I may never understand. And until the day when that question fades to black, I will continue to roar: I am both a mother and a professional, always…and so much more.

Roar

That's How They Always Are

Madison Symes

"Here's my number, so call me maybe…"

An old pop song is playing over the speakers at the bar I am at on a Friday night surrounded by friends. Everyone is singing along and laughing, but I'm spiraling back to another Friday night, five years ago.

Words haunt me. Sentence fragments stick in my memory like gum on a sidewalk – even once you clean it off (I mean, get really into it, down and dirty with the remnants of people passing through) there remains a black, sticky shape to remind you that it once existed, that it will never really leave you. Words bring me back to moments, pull me into memories.

"So call me maybe…Mads, it's our song! Slut, where are you going?"

I turn to face the shouts from the boys' hall in my Gothic-style college dorm. In the doorway, stands a tornado that has been dragging me through a cycle of friendship, assault, dating, rejection, and pursuit for six months – a cycle that will continue for another twelve months after this incident.

"Amber will make out with me whenever I want. What's your problem?"

I am being pushed into a cream cinder block wall. Cream is supposed to be neutral, but soothing – an easy choice for a dorm stairwell. Today was a difficult day, I was crying before, ready for the comfort of these walls I thought I could trust. But neither my puffy eyes nor my hood pulled up around my face seem to discourage the arms holding me in place.

A hand grabs my chin, pinky and ring finger push against my windpipe. I hold my head up, my dead eyes meeting the wild, hungry disks on the face moving towards me, touching mine. I stay perfectly still, count how long I can hold my breath…I reach twelve, breathe, repeat. The body pushes harder against mine. The coarse lips become more aggressive – the corners turning up, a quick laugh creeps across them. My small act of defiance treated as a joke.

My eyes close and I kiss the lips that encapture mine, hoping this will make it end sooner; these lips will get bored and I can disappear into my room like I was trying to do before I was caught sneaking up the stairs. The backs of my arms start to notice the cold ridges on the wall – poking, digging, long fingers hurting places they do not have a right to. The lips are wet and parted while the tongue, with the help of a firm thumb, forces itself into my clenched mouth.

Maybe I am fed up with this day or maybe my instincts kick in – engaged for my protection. My body acts when I cannot. My hands push out against the chest pinned to mine. My legs spin to the right as my torso crouches to escape the cage that is made by someone else's body. As I flee towards the doorway that leads into the hall on my left, my back is to the staircase, which spirals down to the basement. But the cage is fast, too. Two hands grasp my shoulders before pushing backwards. My feet are searching for something solid while the hands release me down the stairs. I am grabbing at the banister, the air.

The hands that did this to me now save me. The arms that pinned me down now pull me back from the air – delivering me from the more immediate danger and back into the chest I had tried to escape.

Cutting through my confusion, a voice enters from the hallway: "Is everything alright with them? Is she okay?"

A young woman who is more concerned than anyone around is looking out for me, asking this group of college students getting ready for their night out to be more aware. She plants a seed for me – this is not normal.

Roar

Reverberating from the cold cinder block walls, the response of a close friend echoes in my memory,

"Everything is fine. That's how they always are…"

"I am sorry."

We are sitting on the stairs that almost shattered my body. I am apologizing. I am sorry, I say to the collared shirt on the arm whose weight is now wrapped around my shoulder, whose buttons I almost ripped off while scrambling for a hold on something, anything. I am sorry, I say to the shoes that I scuffed when I stomped on them, the shoes – I am being told – that cost more than the feet that wear them make in a month at a part-time job.

When I look at that stairwell now – five years in the future – I still say I am sorry. But no longer to the man who decided he had a right to control me and my body. Now I speak to the young woman sitting on those steps apologizing to someone for not allowing them to hurt her. I am sorry this happened to you. I am sorry that you feel alone and guilty. I am not sorry for the strength and resilience that will carry you through this. You were ready to hear new words. You deserved to hear your own words. I am not sorry for those new words you will learn to say.

"I am not sorry."

Amulet

Magin LaSov Gregg

I wore ballet slippers the day I learned to lie. The slippers cusped my white tights, not yet marred by grass stains and snags. Above the tights, I wore a black leotard. I thought I looked like the ballerina figurine in a jewelry box I had once given my mother. The ballerina stood firm on salmon-colored silk, beside a mirror made of foil. She planted one leg solidly against her thigh and rooted the other one to the ground. I loved to open the jewelry box, wind the music key, and watch the ballerina twirl. Her determination drew me to her.

On the day of my first ballet lesson, I attempted the toy ballerina's posture. My mother stood against a floor-to-ceiling mirror that reflected a dozen other whirling ballerinas.

"I need to tell you something," she said, and called me toward her. When I reached her side, she spoke in her I-mean-business-voice. I'd heard this harsh and urgent tone before. She'd used it the morning she told me I should never go with my father if he tried to pick me up from school.

Roar

"If anybody asks, say you're four," my mother whispered, eyeing the ballet teacher, who had turned her back to us.

I was not quite four, which I told her.

"You have to be four to take ballet."

My mother knelt on the floor, and I lowered my head to the shoulder pad of her blazer. I could smell the Dove soap she used to wash her face, and faint notes of rainwater shampoo. I knew she was asking me to lie, and that lying was something I was not supposed to do, a deed akin to hitting my sister or refusing to eat wormy spaghetti. My mother explained the lie was a white lie. White lies were like white magic. We told them to help ourselves. She reminded me of Glinda in *The Wizard of Oz*, a film we watched constantly on the sagging sofa my father left behind after he moved out. If there were good witches and bad witches, it could be the same for lies.

I had no reason to doubt her. She had never lied to me. If someone in ballet class asked my age, I knew I'd say "four" without thinking twice. But no one did. And, after a few weeks of pirouettes that made my back ache, I decided I didn't like ballet. I don't know what happened to the tights or leotard, but my mother kept the ballet slippers in her dresser drawer for 18 years. They were the only clothing from my childhood she did not throw away. I like to think those shoes revealed a glimmer of the girl I used to be, the spark of a child who leapt unafraid through air and space.

The year of my first ballet class was also the year my mother brought her boyfriend, Chance, home. He was the first man she dated after she changed the locks on my father. Chance was the thinnest man I'd ever seen, and the palest. His skin had the pallor of chalk dust. As if to oppose his complexion, black hair sloped across his forehead and hung over his eyes, which were ice blue. He smelled of nutmeg and night air, and I crawled into his lap not a minute after meeting him. I was always crawling onto the laps of my uncles and grandfathers. I thought all men's laps were for me, and Chance didn't mind. He moved his hands through my hair, then over my ears, where he stopped to caress the lobes. But I did not think of Chance's touch as different. I liked the attention. My father rarely held me.

When I was six, I awoke one morning to Chance on top of me. Baby, baby, he moaned in the grainy, pre-dawn light. Now I think he meant the word both ways. Baby, baby for the little girl I was. Baby, baby for the body he fetishized. That morning, I opened my mouth to scream, but no sound came out.

Held against him I could see the pores on his nose. They looked like tiny bugs. I glanced at the faces of Bert and Ernie on my Sesame Street sheets. Their eyes were wide and friendly. I stayed focused on them as Chance's stubble scraped my cheek. I thought of my old ballet slippers, how strong and determined they had once made me feel, like the ballerina in my mother's jewelry box. By this time my shoes were long beyond my reach, hidden beneath sweaters in my mother's dresser.

She slept in a bed beside that dresser in a room down the hall. I did not think to scream for her. I did not know I should. I went as limp as an animal pretending to be dead. I believed my fake paralysis would make Chance retreat. But his mouth moved over my stomach, and to the place my underwear covered. I became quieter than darkness, more stagnant than air. I closed my eyes and disappeared.

Only after he left my bed, did I dare open my eyes to see sunlight filling the room. This was a dream, I thought, lying to myself until I could alchemize my memory of his mouth on my skin, until I could turn it to smoke or fog. If it were all a dream, I could pretend nothing had happened. I could stay silent. I could ignore the stabbing pain in my stomach and walk downstairs, past the bedroom where my mother slept undisturbed in her bed. I could pour myself a bowl of Corn Flakes. I could walk toward the light of another ordinary morning where I went to school and ignored the nausea swimming through me.

To this day, I don't like to think of Chance, but I could not avoid remembering him one June afternoon, when I was in my early thirties. It was the first hot day of late spring. My legs were bare beneath my ruffled skirt, which flared tutu-like over my hips. Earlier in the day, I'd caught my reflection in a full-length mirror and shuddered because I believed the skirt made my hips look fat. But what I remember most is the sky: milk-blue with wispy clouds swirled in, like ribbons of spun sugar. I was looking up at those delicious clouds when a man yelled, Baby! I didn't bother to look at him. I didn't think he could be calling out to me. This was a college campus, not a street corner.

Baby! Baby! The man kept yelling. Without meeting his gaze, I shifted the keys in my hand so they pointed outward like a weapon, my left index finger poised on the launch button of my pepper spray.

Baby! He shouted again. And this time my eyes met his. The man stood between a Goodwill bin and an empty Ryder truck with the cabin open wide, like an eager mouth. The closer I came, the more excited he became.

You look gorgeous today. His lips curled into a smile as he spoke.

For the smallest, hair-split second, I felt a thrill. I felt better about my hips and the skirt that magnified them. I soaked up his attention, let it feed my appetite for approval. Then, as strongly as I'd felt the thrill, I felt dread: this could be a trap. The man could be luring me into his van. My right hand rose to my collar bone. I felt for the rape whistle I wear when I run and bike around my neighborhood. But my whistle was at home, dangling from its perch beside my front door. I had never thought to bring a rape whistle to work.

Thank you. I shouted in a voice I did not recognize immediately as mine.

My lie flew from me like paper swept up by wind. I wanted to retrieve the words as soon as they left my mouth. I wanted to scream, Speak to me with respect! But I silenced myself to get as far away as possible and to avoid a scene. I walked quickly toward my office, breathing in the smell of trash. I went back to the child I used to be, the girl who played dead while Chance overtook her.

Like the girl I once was, I chose a lie of silence because I believed it would protect me. Sometimes I still choose silence when a man shouts at me on the street, or stands too close to me in a grocery store line, his hot breath pooling on the back of my neck. I stay silent because I am afraid. I stay silent because I don't want to be rude. I stay silent because Chance told me he'd hit me if I didn't stop talking. I stay silent because of all the times I heard him talk of killing random strangers, men who cut him off in traffic and women who disobeyed him. My silence is as reflexive as my own breath. Long ago, I accepted the lie that it was better to be courteous than to hurt a man's feelings. I learned to push my own anger as far down as it could go, so far until I could not find the part of me that longed to rage.

After the Goodwill encounter, I resumed control of my body and mind. I inhaled through my nose. I held my breath in the back of my throat and counted to three before releasing the air through my mouth. I watched the branches on the Sycamore tree outside my office window bend in the wind. I noticed how the tree's trunk stayed firmly rooted, and I felt a modicum of comfort. I repeated a calming mantra: Breathe in peace. Breathe out guilt.

What did I feel guilty for? Saying thank you? Baring my legs? Feeling momentarily validated when the Goodwill Man noticed me? Needing to be noticed by a man?

I needed to be absolved, so I called my friend Kay. Her office was down the hall, but I was not ready to make the walk. I thought of Kay as my Work Mom, and I left no detail out about the Goodwill Man story. I knew telling her would make me feel better. Telling always has a way of wiping clean the muck my lies leave in their wake.

"Do I need to tell Mark?" I asked her. Mark was our boss. I worried about the Goodwill Man harassing other women. I wanted to report the incident to a supervisor.

"Don't tell him you said 'Thank you,'" Kay said. I suspected she worried how Mark might hear my "thank you."

In truth, I worried, too. When I've complained on Facebook about being a catcall target, my grievances have been received with mixed reviews. My senior citizen aunts have told me to lighten up: catcalls are compliments, and I should receive them as such. They've written, "I wish someone would catcall me."

I was also ashamed of a small thing I could not deny. The Goodwill Man's words had sent a spark of delight through me. I knew this was how I was supposed to feel. The man had not called me ugly or a bitch. And yet, his "You look gorgeous today," was not a true compliment. The moment the spark faded, so too did the heady rush that had accompanied it. I was left trembling in my skin, transported to a morning my body could not forget.

Like many survivors of childhood sexual abuse, I mistrusted my reactions to men, my memory of events. Did it really happen? I wondered on the morning I awoke to Chance in my bed. Was it a dream? Although I remember Chance entering my bedroom and rousing me from sleep on other occasions, my memory fades to black when I try to probe for further details.

Telling my sister what I recalled of the morning Chance entered my bedroom did not bring the kind of catharsis I expected, not even when she confirmed hearing him enter my bedroom, then said "I always suspected he was abusing you." Her affirmation did not heal my shame or distrust. It simply allowed me to control the only thing I could, which was, ultimately, the narrative. If this were a fairytale and Chance were a villain, then telling my sister would be the amulet that destroyed his power over me. Now, each time I resist a man who behaves as if he is entitled to my body, I erase a mark Chance left on me. I go back to that girl in the bed. I break the spell of her stupor.

Still, my breath caught in my throat as I made the short walk to Mark's office. When I saw him sitting at his desk, I wanted to retreat. I wanted to pretend nothing had happened. But I did not budge. I knew if I said nothing, I'd replay the scene with Goodwill Man in my head all day. I'd tell him off in a million ways. A migraine would pulsate behind my eyes. I'd berate myself. I'd lose sleep.

I'd keep saying "thank you," when I needed to say, "Leave me alone."

I spied the Sycamore tree through Mark's office window. The image gave me a beat of courage. Be the tree, I thought, then divulged everything.

"Why did you thank him?" Mark asked, once I finished.

His eyes tightened at the corners as he spoke. He seemed genuinely baffled. He knew me as a woman who did not stumble over language. But I stood there in front of him barely able to speak. I wish I'd said: Why does it matter what I said? I wish I'd talked about victim blaming and all its tired tropes, or that I'd described my own human resources training at this very institution, where an actress wearing a short skirt, low-cut blouse and high heels played the dual role of Office Slut and Sexual Harassment Victim.

In the parking lot, I had felt desire and fear coursing through me. I could not deny the thrill that ignites inside me when a man sees me. It is the same thrill I felt when Chance gave me toys he didn't give my sister – a ball, a radio, a typewriter. I am visible. I am special. I matter.

"I was scared," I told Mark quickly. "I wasn't thinking."

I knew my "thank you" was an easy lie born of conditioning I wore like second skin, but how could I explain this to Mark? I felt as if I'd failed in an indiscernible but all-encompassing way. I walked back to my office and slumped over my desk. I did not bother to glance up at the tree. I was present, but not. I was there and somewhere else.

That night I went home and looked "catcall" up in the Oxford English Dictionary. I started with cat which derives from the Old English catt, and enters our language in 700 CE to describe a domesticated feline. Cat assumes a connotative meaning in the thirteenth century; this meaning expresses disdain for women. Prostitute. Whore.

Call enters English through the Germanic kall. Its Proto-Indo-European root is gal, which means to scream, shriek, and shout.

As a compound noun, catcall enters common usage in the late seventeenth century to describe an instrument used in English playhouses. A catcall expressed a rare disapprobation that warranted an animalistic shriek, or caterwauling. At its etymological core, catcall is the exact opposite of a compliment, despite what my aunts have told me. I like to imagine the wail of early catcalls as the auditory equivalent of a punch to the face, an affront to the ears and senses, not unlike a modern-day rape whistle.

Now I think about blowing into a catcall the next time a man yells, baby, baby at me. I imagine women worldwide uniting with catcalls each time a man follows us around a supermarket to comment on our rear ends, or tells us to "smile," or yells "baby, baby, baby" from a rolled-down car window. The shriek of the reclaimed catcall could be the sound of our collective silence siphoned to a single, unrepressed note. It is the loudest, most effective fuck you ever whistled.

Ten months after the Goodwill Man encounter, a man I'd seen once or twice but never actually met, stopped by my office. He blocked the doorway and told a joke that ended in a punchline involving penile length. (Women were the sex-crazed idiots in this joke.) The young woman sitting in my office let out a nervous laugh. Her laugh was like my "thank you." A reflexive lie, uttered to protect this man's feelings at the expense of her own. He seemed oblivious to the fact he had just insulted us both.

"In all honesty, I don't find that funny," I told the man.

I did not have to think about these words. They rose without stopping, as effortless as breath. The man lowered his head and scurried away with his shoulders sloped. He has not returned, and I don't expect he will.

After my mother died, my sister took her jewelry box. But I held onto my old ballet slippers. I keep them in a drawer beside my bed. My shoes still smell of sweat and dust and baby powder. I can hold each one in the palm of my hand, fit my wrist inside each gritty sole. A grey patina covers the pink leather, but persistent streaks of color shine against the grime. When I hold them, I remember how these shoes once, so easily, slipped onto my feet, how natural they felt against my heels and toes; I think, too, of the morning I told my best friend about Chance, and she nodded and said, "That's scary." I felt relief dissolve my shame. When I demanded to sleep in my sister's room, I knew my voice could protect me. My words could forge an antidote against harm, the one amulet strong enough to break a lie.

Mary's Rock

Kim O'Connell

Don't walk alone. Don't talk to strangers. Don't make eye contact.

I know all the rules, the ones you learn to follow when you are young. The ones you learn the hard way, like I did. Like so many women do.

I broke the rules once and paid the price. For a long time, I was afraid of the consequences of breaking those rules. It would take more fear, not less, to help me change the rules that governed how I lived.

***

It was the mid-1990s. I was 24 and living on my own for the first time on the sixth floor of a dingy corner apartment building near Dupont Circle in Washington, D.C. My unit overlooked both an alley and the swankier building next door, which managed to give me regular views of both elegant dinner parties and overstuffed dumpster rats.

He'd seemed nice enough. It was a balmy summer night, and I was standing in line at my local Safeway grocery store. Like other D.C. Safeways, my neighborhood grocery had been given a nickname – the "Soviet Safeway" – so designated because of its penchant for long lines and empty shelves. (The Safeway in the hipper Georgetown neighborhood was called the "Social Safeway," which sounded infinitely better.) As I waited in line, the man standing behind me struck up a conversation. The Soviet Safeway suddenly became more social.

He was tall, dark-haired, and good looking. So, I made eye contact. I talked to a stranger. I didn't give him my name. But, at some point, I casually mentioned that I was an editorial assistant at a certain association magazine. Then I paid for my ramen and cereal and walked into the night.

The next day, he called me at work. He had gone to the library, found a copy of my magazine, and perused the masthead until he found my position and thus my name. I was startled, but flattered. He asked if I wanted to meet him at a nearby fountain, just to get to know each other better. I agreed.

I don't remember what we talked about, but I remember that there was something about him that made me nervous. Maybe it was the way he leaned in too closely when he talked. Or how he used "we" too soon. Or the way he smiled too eagerly, like it was some kind of dare. Whatever it was, after a while I feigned some excuse and departed, thinking that the city was big enough for both of us, and that I would probably never see him again.

I was wrong. Unbeknownst to me, he followed me home. He showed up outside my apartment after that, startling me when I left to go to the grocery store or the office. He waited for me outside my workplace and walked me home. (We lived in the same neighborhood, after all, he would say.) He found my home number and began calling me regularly. He was always unfailingly polite, feigning surprise or ignorance when I said he was making me nervous or asked him to stop contacting me. When I finally threatened to call the police, he laughed, because he seemed to know that I wouldn't.

And I never did. I had brought this situation on myself. I had broken the rules of engagement and invited his interest in the grocery store. Because I took the blame, I felt powerless. He seemed like he was everywhere, then, even when he wasn't. In the grocery store, on the Metro, at the fountain. I saw his face on perfect strangers. Even years afterwards, the memory of him would sometimes come back to haunt me, reminding me to stay guarded, to follow the rules to stay safe.

***

Still, I was surprised when his image returned recently, like an unexpected house guest, as I was standing at a trailhead in Shenandoah National Park. It was a mild September morning, the cool air signaling that summer was finally loosening its grip. Red-shouldered hawks circled above me, and here and there, leaves had begun to change color. It was the first day of a two-week solo stay as the park's artist-in-residence, a gift of time and space to write, hike, and breathe, far from the demands of normal life. For my first solo hike, I chose a six-mile trek to Mary's Rock, a 3,514-foot summit in the park's central district.

I knew from my guidebook that the trail would go up through a series of switchbacks and ascents until one reached a rocky overlook facing west, with a panoramic view of the surrounding Blue Ridge Mountains and the quilted farmland of the valley far below. It's not one of the park's highest or hardest hikes, but it possessed a scenic pay-off and seemed like a good place to start.

Yet plunging into the bower-darkened woods, even on that crystalline morning, seemed antithetical to everything I'd been taught about the world. I was an avid hiker, but I'd almost never hiked alone, and not in such a rugged terrain, far from the known confines of my normal life. Anxiety suddenly gripped me by the shoulders, confronting me with the ghosts of my past. I remembered the time when a drunken man had blocked my passage and hurled salacious comments at me on the train, tugging at my skirt, while my fellow riders said nothing and stared at their shoes. Another time, when I was younger, a strange man wearing latex gloves chased me and a friend down a bike trail. We managed to escape unharmed, but not long after, a woman was found strangled on that same path. The perpetrator was never caught.

And then there was my stalker, whose incessant, insistent friendliness had made me wonder whom I could really trust. Years had gone by, and I could still picture him, could still recall that fear of wondering if he'd be there when I turned the next corner.

Don't walk alone. Don't talk to strangers. Don't make eye contact.

Intellectually, I knew that he wasn't likely to be on that trail in Shenandoah. In fact, I hadn't seen him, except in my mind, in two decades. After a few weeks of calls and run-ins, he had simply stopped pursuing me. Maybe he found another quarry; maybe something happened to him. I don't want to know. I moved to a new place in Virginia, with a new grocery store. I felt some measure of relief that that chapter had closed. In some ways, it hadn't. The world hadn't gotten safer; I simply grew protective plates of armor, like some prehistoric creature. I stopped walking alone and talking to strange men. I filled my life with work and family and travel, but I usually stayed in my comfort zone. I followed the rules.

Like so many women, I have spent years conflating caution and politeness with safety, not realizing that playing it safe wasn't always that safe after all. In fact, I was only teaching myself how to stay afraid.

I didn't want to be afraid in Shenandoah, even though I was – of strange men, of bears, of fear itself. I decided that, if I was going to be afraid, I might as well carry the fear with me. Maybe, I thought, I would gain something by gathering the things that scared me closer rather than pushing them away. Maybe I would find the power I had ceded long ago. I took a deep breath and started walking.

***

According to local legend, Mary's Rock was named after Mary Savage, who once lived in a mountain hollow nearby. Another tale claimed that a scrappy young girl named Mary climbed this mountain and came back clutching a bear cub under her arm. Whoever she was, as an antidote to my fear, I tried to imagine the mythical Mary as a guiding spirit, protecting the mountain – mother, sister, companion, to me and all the souls who would come after me. The patron saint of solo hikers. I kept walking.

But my anxiety didn't abate as I moved down the trail. In fact, my heart pounded so loudly that I imagined it was scaring birds out of their nests. I started to make more noise, to alert any predators to my presence and to distract me from my anxiety. I banged my hiking staff against boulders. When I heard a rustling noise a few yards off-trail, I unholstered my bear mace, which I had test-sprayed at home so I wouldn't accidentally incapacitate myself. I even belted out show tunes. The lyrics of one song in particular, "Broadway, Here I Come," seemed strangely fitting:

I'm standing on the ledge

The view from here is pretty

and I step off the edge

I eventually reached a clearing, where I stopped to catch my breath and grabbed a drink of water. After a few moments, a man burst into view from the trail from which I had just emerged, bearing a full pack and carrying twin hiking sticks.

Has he been walking behind me this whole time? Did he hear me singing? Will he hurt me?

"Hi," he said, as he walked past me.

"Hi," I responded.

I watched his back disappear into the woods beyond the clearing, towards Mary's Rock. He never even gave me a second glance, and yet I decided I'd had enough. I turned back towards the trailhead. The ghosts had won.

***

Back at the start, I felt angry at myself for turning around, for making so much noise in the quiet woods, and most of all for letting my fear get the better of me. I made a vow, in that moment, to never turn back again.

I hiked every day during my time in Shenandoah. It wasn't always easy, and I was often scared, but I never turned back. Every day, I felt a little stronger, in body and in will, and less afraid. I hiked down to Lewis Falls and climbed the rock scramble at Bearfence Mountain, with its dizzying 360-degree view. I followed a fire road to the remnants of an early 20th century Protestant mission, where I found old gravestones and a staircase leading nowhere, where the presence of the past felt potent and real. One misty morning, as I traced the lines of a former Civilian Conservation Corps camp in a meadow, I stumbled across a family of deer feeding on the dewy grass. To my amazement, the stag let me approach, and our eyes locked together for a long, weighted moment before he turned and bolted.

During my two-week stay, however, I never went back to Mary's Rock. Something, maybe shame, stopped me from revisiting the trail where I'd met my stalker, or at least the idea of him. But I had come a long way. After I re-entered my normal life, whether I was in the woods or in a room full of strangers, I began to welcome the ghosts I felt all around me – the kindred spirits, the brave souls, like the stag, like Mary. I began to feel that I was a brave soul, too, ready to toss out the old cautionary rules like outgrown shoes. Mary, my patron saint, had not let me down. I know now that I can climb mountains. I can confront the past and face the unknown. I can bring back a bear under my arm or in my heart.

A few months ago, I found myself passing through Shenandoah again. This time, I was determined. I pulled over at the trailhead to Mary's Rock. In a forest ablaze with autumn foliage, I hiked alone to the summit, listening to my breath, feeling the sun warm my skin, greeting other hikers I met along the way. At the top, I gave a silent thanks to the world for being so mysterious and strange and beautiful, so that I might be brave enough to discover it, ghosts and all.

The Interrupted Playdate

Laura Bowman Pimentel

The floor had fallen out from beneath my feet and I was hanging by a thread. I was used to being able to solve things. For myself and for others. At times, my hands would shake and I felt as if I might vomit, but I was able to convince others that I was fine. When I think back to this time, one particular afternoon is seared into my memory as especially absurd and heartbreaking.

Our oldest son had just begun preschool at a great neighborhood charter school. I had been very lonely up to this point. At that time in my life, I didn't have many other friends who had any children, much less a toddler and a new six-month-old baby. I was overwhelmed, but I was also hopeful that some of the new parents at school might become friends. It seemed we had all been feeling rather isolated and were quite desperate to connect and vent about the struggles of parenthood. But as difficult as this phase was, I was facing an even more urgent crisis. On top of the overwhelming challenges of parenting, my marriage and world were coming unraveled.

It was a warm, sunny day and a few of us mothers went to a nearby playground after school to let our kids run free and see if we could forge our own friendships. We made sure the kids were full of snacks and then we let them fly while we savored our sacred adult space. My own mother was in town helping with the baby, so I was free and trying, for one afternoon, to pretend things were completely normal.

But my life was far from normal. My husband was losing his mind. He was in a psychotic state. It had come on little by little, a paranoia that I could initially reason away until it became too extreme. Schizophrenia they said. Thinking that the police were following him, hanging blankets over the windows so no one could see in, checking for his name on the FBI's Most Wanted list, convinced that others were whispering that they thought he was gay. I was confused about what was happening at first and I hoped that it would just go away. But, in the pit of my stomach, I knew that something was very wrong.

A few days earlier, we were driving home with the kids in the car and he declared that he simply couldn't be at home. He felt trapped there and being at home was making him even crazier, he said. I asked him where he wanted to go. He couldn't think of a single place where he would "feel safe". I didn't know what to do, so I called a friend to stay with the boys and took him to the emergency room. He refused to be admitted, but he did agree to talk with a psychiatrist and agreed that he needed medication. The evening was an emotionally exhausting ordeal. Now we were desperately waiting for our appointment with the psychiatrist in the coming week. Once we got the meds and he started taking them, I knew that it could be weeks until they would start taking effect. I couldn't imagine living like this for weeks. Days felt like years at this point.

It was awful to see my husband suffering. He was very scared and didn't understand what was happening to him. During moments of lucidity, he realized that he was being irrational, but lucidity was fleeting. There was no relief for him unless he was sleeping, which sometimes he did virtually all day long. Sometimes sleep eluded him completely. Talking to him felt similar to when you're talking to someone who is distracted by music or the television and not really listening to you. I was in a constant state of fear at what he might do to himself.

I needed the escape of this play date. And so did my son. I accepted the play date invitation with great expectation. Initially, it was exactly what I hoped. The kids were joyous. The moms were bonding. We lamented how much motherhood demanded of us. How little of ourselves we had left. I couldn't help but wonder what these women would think if they knew of everything going on in my life.

After an hour or so, I was actually beginning to feel somewhat normal. Like having to lug that damn infant car seat around everywhere I went was also one of the biggest struggles that I needed to vent about. I was starting to feel a little lighter. And then my phone rang. I saw my husband's name and my stomach flipped. I smiled nervously and excused myself to speak to him. The minute I heard his voice I knew that he wasn't okay.

"They're following me," he whispered. I thought I might throw up.

"Nobody's following you. Where are you?"

"I'm near Children's Hospital. Can you come and get me?"

"How did you get there?"

"I walked." The hospital was miles away. Why did my mom let him leave the house?

"Okay, tell me where you are and I'll come get you now. But listen to me. No one is following you. That's in your head. It's not true, okay?"

"Okay," he responded voice quavering.

I hung up the phone and smiled at my new friends. I didn't want my son to have to stop playing and I really didn't want him to witness his dad this way.

"My husband has locked himself out of the car." I rolled my eyes as if to say, 'you know how husbands can be.' "Do you mind if I leave Benjamin with you while I go give him my key?"

Of course they didn't mind. I hugged my son tightly, holding back tears and trying to look as normal as possible. When I got in the car and pulled away, I let the tears stream down my face. Halfway there, my husband called again.

"Are you close?" he whispered.

"Yes, and you're fine. No one is going to hurt you." When I pulled up to where he said he was, I didn't see anyone. Then he stood up and came out of the bushes where he had been hiding and my heart broke. He was disheveled and unshaven. His eyes were dilated and he looked around nervously. Thank god the police hadn't stopped him. It would've been traumatic for him in this state and only increased the paranoia. He quickly got into the car. I put my hand on his arm and told him that he was okay. I couldn't begin to understand what he was going through. But I also knew that I couldn't continue to go through it with him. And I was horrified by what kind of person that made me.

I continued to speak to him on the drive home and assure him that what he thought had happened wasn't real. He'd been taking a walk and just kept walking for miles without really thinking about where he was going. He'd done this a lot. He was just literally trying to escape his thoughts. Suddenly, he felt that two men were following him. He jumped into the bushes to get away from them and hide. By the time we got home, he seemed to believe that this wasn't real and thanked me for trying to bring him back to reality. We went in the house where my mother was making dinner and our baby was sleeping. My mother didn't say a word after seeing the look on my face. My husband got into bed. His head hurt, he said, and he needed to rest his brain and sleep. Yes, I agreed and tucked him into bed.

With tears that I couldn't stop, I went to kiss my peacefully sleeping baby. I was so afraid for what his and all of our lives were going to be like now. How could we get through it, especially if it never gets better? If he never gets well? I swallowed the fear and focused on how to get through that day, that moment. I couldn't entertain the thought of what would happen to my children if I broke down as well.

When I headed back to pick up my older son, I'm not sure how the mothers could not have noticed my red eyes or shaky voice. But they didn't say a word. My son was playing happily with his new friend who would eventually become one of his best buddies. His mother would become one of my closest friends who, once she knew the truth of what was happening, would give me incredible support and wisdom to navigate what was to come. But for today, the sun was setting and the air was getting chilly. I thanked the women for watching my son and we rounded up the kids who began whining about having to leave.

"Don't worry," we assured them as we hugged goodbye. "It's time to go home now, but we promise we'll have another playdate again soon."

The Talk

Jessica Robinson

"Does it hurt?"

"Does what hurt?"

"You know, *it.* Does *it* hurt? Like, the first time."

My mom and I had "the talk" when I was 8 years old. I'd just watched *Fast Times at Ridgemont High.* My mom was a cool mom. For good or ill, she let me watch whatever I wanted. At 8 years old, the scene where Jennifer Jason Leigh lost her virginity was a little scary. (The abortion stuff went over my head.)

I asked my mom, "Does it hurt?"

She smiled, as if recalling some happy memory and said, "No. Not if you're in love. If he cares about you and you care about him, it doesn't hurt. In fact, it feels good."

Unfortunately, that wasn't the only time we talked about *it.* When I hit the more appropriate age of twelve or thirteen, my mom stopped editing herself and told me many horrifying things about sex, horrifying because they were about my mom having sex. She loved sex, and wanted me to grow up to enjoy it as well. As a grown woman, I am grateful that she instilled in me the idea that sex is something a woman should enjoy. In retrospect, though, I find it strange that, with all the over-sharing, there was one woman-to-woman, mother-to-daughter talk we never had, one story she never shared. My mom, who was perfectly okay explaining to her tween-aged daughter how she worked the penis pump with her boyfriend, never felt comfortable telling me about her rape.

As I grew up, I learned to tune out most of what my mom said about sex. But the talk we'd had when I was 8 stuck with me, became my guide. I wanted my first time to be with someone who cared about me. I didn't realize that was such a high bar to set, yet, at 23 years old, I was still looking.

I was working as a production assistant in the film industry in New York. One night, I went to a wrap party for a movie I'd only worked on for a week. Wrap parties meant free alcohol and I was young. Plus, I liked the crew and wanted to have a night out with the guys before we all moved on to the next movie.

At around midnight, after I'd probably had two or three too many, Jim came up to me at the bar and handed me a drink. I'd never worked with him on any other movies, so

I'd only known him for 6 days. There wasn't much time to talk during work but, whenever we had, he seemed nice. He was soft spoken, tall and thin, and had a boy-next-door sort of charm.

I probably didn't need to take another shot, but why not? I took the glass from Jim and we both drank. Then he pulled me onto the dance floor. He started swinging me around, jitterbug style, and, after maybe a minute, I started to get really dizzy. It was like the world around me was blurring out of focus and I couldn't find my balance. Jim pulled me off the dance floor and out of the bar without giving me a chance to say goodbye to anyone.

I confess, much of the rest of the night is unclear to me. The moments I do recall feel distant, like they were played back for me starring someone else's body, someone else's feelings. But there are gaps, too. In my mind, it's like we cut to the next scene, and then the next. In between is blackness.

Cut.

We were in a cab. I noticed we were driving uptown. I said, "I live in Brooklyn."

Jim put his hand on my leg and told me, "It's okay."

Cut.

Roar

Jim pushed me into his apartment, hand on the small of my back. He didn't turn his lights on and I couldn't see. He kept his hand there, nudging me through the apartment and into his bedroom. As soon as the door closed behind him, he pulled my dress off over my head. It wasn't passionate. We weren't making out and ripping each other's clothes off. He just took my dress off as if it were in his way.

Cut.

We were in his bed. Jim was propped on one arm, holding up a condom. I waved it away, saying, "Whoa, we're not gonna need that."

He smiled, threw it on the ground, and said, "Awesome."

Cut.

Jim was leaning over me, hand between my legs. I said, "I'm a virgin."

Normally, that frightened guys away. Jim just said, "That's great."

I said, "I don't want to do this."

Cut.

Jim was on top of me. He said "Ready?"

Before I could answer, he was inside me. There was a pinch. It hurt.

Cut.

Jim was lying next to me, snoring. I climbed out of bed as quietly as possible, but ended up falling to the ground. The bed was high, stacked on dresser drawers.

Jim continued to snore. I stumbled around the dark room trying to find my underwear, bra, dress, purse and shoes amidst his possessions, scattered across the floor. I didn't turn on the light. I didn't want to wake him.

I got dressed and found his bathroom. As I pulled my underwear down, blood smeared along my thigh. The sight of blood hit me – I was no longer a virgin. I sat on the toilet and cried until I started to worry that he might wake up and find me.

Cut.

I walked out of his apartment and downstairs onto the street, which is when I realized I had no idea where I was. It was 4 a.m. I was still woozy, in last night's dress, and I hadn't brought money for a cab. Absurdly, this was the first moment that night that I remember feeling anger. Jim shouldn't have brought me to his place without planning to get me home. But what could I do? I walked toward an avenue, looking for a subway stop.

Cut.

I got home around 5 a.m. and tried to go to sleep.

I got up not long after, feeling hung-over, sick to my stomach, tired, and incredibly sad. I cried all day. I cried all weekend. I called my mom and cried as I told her I lost my virginity. I told her I was drunk. I told her I hadn't wanted it to happen. I told her I was ashamed.

Mom said, "It's all right. It's over now."

In other words, I should move on. I just didn't feel like I could.

Normally, talking to my mom when I was upset helped. This time, I was even more depressed after I hung up. There was something she wasn't understanding, something I needed for my mom to explain to me, because I didn't understand either. My confusion led to more tears.

I felt sick about what had happened, but couldn't comprehend why it felt so wrong to me. In fact, there were a lot of things about that night I couldn't understand and there was one person who could clear things up for me. Thanks to the crew list, I had his number.

I called Jim on Monday. As soon as he picked up the phone, I wished I hadn't. I felt embarrassed and couldn't even pretend to make small talk. I said, "I never did that before. I didn't want that to happen. I've never done that before."

He said, "I know. It was fun. We had fun."

I don't know what I was expecting him to say. I think I'd wanted him to ask me out, to suggest we were dating, so losing my virginity wouldn't feel so much like a one-night stand. Still, when he said we had fun, a new pit grew in my stomach. Fun? It hadn't felt like fun to me. I needed to get off the phone before I started crying. When I said goodbye, Jim said, "We should hang out soon." I hung up. I never wanted to see him again.

The moment I lost my virginity hurt. There was a pinch. There was blood. There was no going back. What hurt more was Jim telling me we'd had fun. If he'd known I hadn't wanted to have sex, if he'd known how much I hurt, he couldn't possibly have called it fun. He must not have known. I must not have been clear.

Jim gave me an understanding. I was no longer someone who was waiting for the right guy to come along. I was someone who had given it up one drunken night. I felt guilty. Even though I didn't believe that casual sex was immoral, my first time felt wrong to me. For years, I interpreted that as shame.

About ten years later, a few of my girlfriends came over to help me settle into my new, post-divorce house in Northern Virginia. We were all single and so, of course, we started talking about sex, which led to a discussion of our first times. One of my friends had a wonderful experience with a guy she loved. The two others had a similar experience to mine. One had been unconscious in her dorm when it happened. The other had been with her boyfriend and told him she wasn't ready. He hadn't listened. The three of us shared our experiences. None of us used the word rape.

A few weeks later, I was watching TV alone and some dumb movie came on. I kept watching. It was a bad movie kind of a day. There was a scene where this girl got roofied – a scary situation that was making the "news at 11" rounds at the time. The guy who drugged her pulled her out of the bar, took her somewhere, and had sex with her. And then, I found myself on the floor sobbing, having trouble catching my breath.

I recognized what was happening to her. She said no. He didn't listen. She tried to fight but was too out of it to stop him. The movie was clear on one thing – she was raped.

I still don't know if I was drugged or simply very drunk the night I lost my virginity. I know I told Jim I didn't want to do it. I know he didn't stop. I know I was too out of it to put up a fight.

I blamed myself for ten years for getting into that situation, for being drunk, for not screaming or kicking him – for not being clear. If I had been, he wouldn't have hurt me. He would've stopped. He thought we had fun. He must not have known.

Except. Lying there, crying, ten years later, I started to wonder if maybe he had known. Maybe he knew exactly how drunk I was, how helpless I was, how, when I said I was a virgin and didn't want to do it, that I was saying no, even if I didn't scream. Maybe he had fun, despite knowing he hurt me. I won't ever be certain what he was thinking. Only now, I understand. What he did to me was rape, whether or not that's what he thought he was doing. I was raped.

When I called my mom that weekend and told her what had happened, she told me it was over. She didn't say, "it wasn't your fault." She didn't say "what he did to you was wrong." She said it was over. It's been nearly twenty years now, and I'm okay, but it's not over.

I don't blame my mom. She loved me. She wished I wasn't in pain. She wanted me to bury what had happened and move on, the way I found out later she had done. That's what women do. They don't talk about rape. They don't blame anyone else. It never occurred to my mom to tell me that it wasn't my fault.

In the nearly ten years since my revelation, since that dumb movie changed my thinking, I still have not told the story of my rape. Thinking about that night makes me uncomfortable. Even using that word is hard for me. I don't want to talk about it. I want to move on and forget it ever happened. I can't.

The world has not changed, has not gotten better. Boys still do bad things to girls. But in the last ten years, my life has changed. I have become a mother. I have one boy and one girl. They are my world, and I would do anything to keep them from getting hurt.

I hope I'm a cool mom, like my mom was. I hope that my kids feel like they can ask me anything. I hope I don't embarrass them too much.

One day, I will have "the talk" with each of them.

When I talk to my son about having sex for the first time, I will discuss consent and double standards and love. But, for the most part, what my mom told me works well as a guide for my boy. "Make sure that you care about the person, and that they care about you, and then, it won't hurt."

Unfortunately, I have learned that that is not enough to say to my daughter. I will need to warn her, tell her the rules of survival, things my son most likely doesn't need to learn. Boys get hurt too, I know that. In the world we live in, however, girls get hurt more.

Much of the hurt that happens is unavoidable. Sometimes, however, a situation could turn out differently, if a person is properly warned. And so, I will tell both my son and my daughter the story of my rape and hope that it is enough to keep the hurt away.

And if my daughter ever comes to me and tells me that she was drunk, or unconscious, that she thought she said no but she's not sure, if my daughter ever cries in pain, if she ever tells me it hurt and felt wrong, then I will take her in my arms and tell her, "It's over. You're okay. It wasn't your fault."

Author Biographies

Laura Bowman Pimentel originally hails from Lancaster County, Pennsylvania, but has lived in the DC area for the past 17 years. In addition to writing whenever she can, Laura is the mom of two amazing boys, a full-time real estate agent and a part-time food tour guide. She loves cooking and exploring the DC restaurant scene, as well as taking in great art of all genres. Her personal blog – www.yourdcabode.com – highlights her explorations around Washington, DC. Laura served as a Peace Corps volunteer in the Dominican Republic, which is where she met her ex-husband and father of her children. Her experience with her husband's struggle to adjust to life in the United States and the resulting mental health consequences have inspired her to speak out and dispel myths about both mental illness and immigration.

Courtney Crane writes stories about coming of age in the South, parenting teens, and adventures in "La-La Land". Her work was featured in the "Expressing Motherhood" Downtown L.A. 2015 & Southbay 2016 shows, and in the "Listen to Your Mother" 2016 Burbank show. She participates in the annual NOHO Lit Crawl with her beloved writing group, Ladies Who Lit. Courtney grew up in New Orleans and lives in Los Angeles with her husband, two teenagers, and oversized rescue dog. When she's not writing stories or wrangling her family, Courtney works for an art consultancy and an artsy boutique. This is her first published piece.

Elizabeth Futrell works to improve access to voluntary family planning and reproductive health services among underserved populations. As the Content Development Lead for the Knowledge for Health (K4Health) Project at The Johns Hopkins Center for Communication Programs, she sees storytelling as a critical means of health communication. In 2015, Liz and her colleagues at

K4Health and Family Planning 2020 founded Family Planning Voices (fpvoices.org), a global storytelling initiative in support of contraceptive access that has published stories from individuals in more than 50 countries. Find her writing via *Medium* (@elizabethfutrell) and *I Ate the Spider*, a decade-old writing collaborative resurfacing in 2017 as a quarterly live event. Prior to earning her Master of Science in Public Health, Liz was a Peace Corps volunteer in Morocco and an English teacher in Japan and the US. She lives in Chicago with her husband and two daughters.

Susan Gordon is a storyteller, published poet, and a prose writer of memoir and fiction. She is a skilled teller of traditional tales and has taught storytelling in colleges, universities, and from the barn on her farm. Susan is now telling personal stories that explore the weave of relationships in her life. She hosts the Hilltop Writers, is asked to read her poetry in a range of settings, and offers a series of house concerts from her home. Susan has a master's degree in narrative therapies and lives with her dog, River, in Frederick County, Maryland.

Sheila Grinell moved to Phoenix, Arizona, in 1993 to serve as founding CEO of the Arizona Science Center. Toward the end of her forty-year career in the science museum field, she began to write fiction. Her debut novel, *Appetite*, was published in May 2016. Born in a taxi in Manhattan, she studied at the Bronx High School of Science, Harvard University, and the University of California, Berkeley. She lives in Phoenix with her husband and spirited dog. To learn more, visit sheilagrinell.com.

Dawn Gross, MD, PhD is a mother, wife, sister, and daughter, writer and hospice and palliative medicine physician practicing at the University of California, San Francisco. When not caring for patients, she can be heard on the radio as host of "Dying To Talk," on 91.7FM KALW, the first of its kind, live-call-in program dedicated to transforming the taboo around talking about death. Her writing has appeared in several journals including *The New York Times*, *JAMA*, *Science*, and *Annals of Internal Medicine*. She is an invited storyteller and hard at work on her first book. Learn more at www.drasyouwish.com.

Sandra Hull has long used storytelling in her day job as an eLearning Instructional Designer, but only recently embraced storytelling to entertain and educate live audiences with her personal experiences and truths. She's been a member of Better Said Than Done, a Fairfax, Virginia-based storytelling troupe, since 2015. Previously, she performed with a handful of DC-area amateur improv troupes and was a regularly published contestant in humor-writing contests in *The Washington Post*, *The Toronto Globe and Mail*, and *New York Magazine*. When not telling stories, Sandra practices active listening as a volunteer with Woman Within International, a non-profit organization that encourages women to support each other in fully living the lives they want.

Bushra Jabre is Associate Faculty, Senior Communication Advisor of The Johns Hopkins Center for Communication Programs/ Bloomberg School of Public Health. She was the Project Director of *Arab Women Speak Out* and the Emerging Leadership Project. She directed the annual Arabic Advances in Development Communication Regional Workshop 1992-2006. She provided technical assistance to health communication programs in the near East and North Africa, Central Asian Republics, West Africa, and the South Pacific Islands, as well as regional initiatives in the Arab World. She held the post of Regional Advisor in Health Education and Women's Programs with the UNICEF Regional Office for the Middle East and North Africa in Amman, Jordan. She published *Sophie's Book*, a memoir about her mother, in 2016, *Arab Women*

Speak Out in 1998, *Emerging Leadership in the Arab World* in 2004, and many technical articles and books and several articles in newspapers in Arabic, English, and French.

Cheryl Kanuck was born and raised in upstate New York, in a peaceful suburb of the city of Albany, and now lives in South Carolina's beautiful "lowcountry". Cheryl is retired from a career as an addiction therapist and program director, and resides in an active adult community with her husband. She says, "I usually write for pleasure (sometimes poetry just for fun), for 'personal therapy' and to preserve genealogical family history. The story included in this volume was written for therapy, to exorcise a demon that was sucking the life from my child, by writing about my own pain. In the living and in the writing, I unearthed a strength I didn't know I had. By my sharing, I hope other women will see their own strength reflected."

Urmilla Khanna, a board-certified pediatrician, came to the United Sates as a young bride in 1963 and pursued her medical career until 2000. After her retirement, she began to write as a hobby, soon to realize that it was her passion. Besides publishing her essays in newspapers and magazines, she has published two of her short stories in *Patchwork: Stories from the Dining Table*. Her first book, *Boundaries of the Wind* – a memoir, was published in 2015, and is available on Amazon in both Kindle and print editions.

Magin LaSov Gregg's writing has appeared in *The Washington Post*, *The Huffington Post*, *The Rumpus*, *Hippocampus Magazine*, *River Teeth's Beautiful Things*, and other publications. *Proximity Magazine* named her as a finalist in its 2016 inaugural Personal Essay Prize. She lives with her husband Carl and their four rescue pets.

Mary Nicol Lucas is a marketing consultant to the credit union industry. Her areas of expertise include name development and rebranding; creation of advertising materials, collateral, website development and public relations. She started her marketing career with the advertising agency J. Walter Thompson USA, and she worked for DDB Needham Worldwide before spending 19 years as a corporate Director of Sales and Marketing for CORT, a Berkshire Hathaway Company.

Judy Nicastro grew up in New Jersey and became political at the age of 14 when her father died and Congress repealed a law that guaranteed college to children whose parents died. She got angry, and worked her way through college at the University of Washington and then graduated University of Washington School of Law. Wanting to make a difference and represent the working class, she ran for political office and won a citywide seat in Seattle as a City Councilmember, representing over 550,000 people. No longer in public office, she hosts a podcast called, "Mayberry with Highrises." She gives speeches and writes articles. She has been printed in *The New York Times*, *The Seattle Times*, and other publications. Her husband and 2 children remind her every day that being silly and having courage make for a beautiful life.

Kim O'Connell is a writer based in Arlington, Virginia, whose articles and essays have appeared in national and regional publications including *The New York Times*, *The Washington Post*, *Brain, Child*, *Babble*, *Yahoo News*, *Ladies Home Journal*, *National Parks*, *PsychologyToday.com*, *Thread*, and more. Her short fiction and poetry have appeared in *Little Patuxent Review* and *unFold Poetry*, and she has been a writer in residence at the Virginia Center for the Creative Arts and at Shenandoah National Park. Her website is www.kimaoconnell.com.

Jessica Robinson is a storyteller with, and the founder of, Better Said Than Done (bettersaidthandone.com), a storytelling organization in Fairfax, Virginia, with monthly, themed storytelling shows featuring true, personal stories, and with storytelling workshops for non-profits, corporations, and individuals. Jessica's first novel, the urban fantasy *Caged*, was published in October 2016, under the pen name JP Robinson (jprobinsonwriter.com). Jessica is currently working on the sequel, *Rise*, due out this summer. Her true, personal story, "The Game," was published in the short story collection *Sucker for Love*, and "What Are the Odds" was published in *The Northern Virginia Review*, Volume 29.

Erin Rodgers is a storyteller, writer, and workshop facilitator from Toronto, Canada. She coaches storytelling, writing and creativity and has taught workshops on both. As a comedy performer and storyteller, Erin performs across Canada and in the US. She is the proud creator of storytelling shows *Storystar* and *Awkward*. Her one-person storytelling show, *Tough*, was featured in The Toronto Storytelling Festival and the Winnipeg Fringe.

Danielle Stonehirsch has been reading and writing all her life. For the last three years, she has worked with the Youth Service Opportunities Project as the Program Director in Washington, DC, managing educational programs which engage youth in volunteer service to the homeless and hungry. Her B.A. in literature comes from Washington University in St. Louis, and she now lives with her beloved husband in Silver Spring, Maryland. She is grateful to her family for their love and support.

Mary Supley Foxworth tells true, personal stories with Better Said Than Done and leads workshops in the art of storytelling. Though she has been an editor of and contributor to other non-fiction books, her story in *Roar* is her first credit as an author. She enjoys writing recipes and is working on a cookbook.

Madison Symes lives in Washington, DC, with her best friends and a large cat, comically named Nugget.

Anne B. Thomas is the 2013 National Storytelling Festival Slam Champion. Her storytelling has been featured on national U.S. storytelling programs such as The Moth, Storycorps, and RISK!. She has been published in *The New York Times* and is a coauthor of the book, *Sucker For Love.* Anne spent most of her career as a civil rights attorney, conflict resolution expert, and leadership development innovator. She is currently writing a memoir that will be published in 2018. You can learn more about Anne at her website, annebthomas.com.

Daya Wakens is a member of the Writers Like Writers Group, and her writing projects are primarily humanitarian concerns. Daya's "Wisdomgram" was published in the "Wayfarers All," November 2013 issue of the *American Athenaeum* literary journal, and her short story, "Embraced with Clarity," is published in *Break the Cycle Volume III*, published by Kathy Chaffin Gerstorff in 2016. Persistence and the power to rise above changed her journey into living life to its fullest with her wonderful husband and family.

Acknowledgements
By Jessica Robinson

I and the authors of this book would like to thank everyone who contributed to bringing *Roar* to print.

Firstly, thanks to the panel of reviewers who selected the stories featured herein: Mary Lucas, Meredith Maslich, Richard Peabody and Mary Supley Foxworth.

A special thank you to Mary Lucas and Mary Supley Foxworth who put in so much of their time providing valuable feedback to the authors, and helping, in general, with the editing process.

Thank you to Bart Robinson for the beautiful cover design and for creating the Roar logo – for the storytelling show, this book and for any future roaring we might like to do.

Thank you to Alex Dixon for connecting me with the National Network to End Domestic Violence. I am glad to be working with NNEDV on this project and to be doing my small part in helping them raise funds and awareness. Thank you to Morgan Dewey at NNEDV for her assistant throughout the process.

I am sure, like me, all of the authors have various writing partners or support groups that they would like to thank. The list would fill a book so, suffice it to say, thank you to everyone who has contributed to supporting the authors and their writing.

Finally, I would like to personally thank all of the authors for sharing their stories. Thank you for opening your hearts and for opening our eyes. You are helping to change the world, one roar at a time.

Made in the USA
Middletown, DE
16 February 2020